Rekindled

"In *Rekindled*, Mallory Smyth shares her experience of being Catholic, why she left, and how she returned to the Church to find far more depth than initially met her eye. This book will become a great aid in helping others find the fullness of joy in the Catholic Church!"

Sarah Swafford
Catholic speaker and author of *Emotional Virtue*

"*Rekindled* is a gripping story about how we should move past surface-level deficiencies in the Catholic Church and embrace the beauty of Catholicism's timeless truths. I highly recommend it."

Trent Horn
Staff apologist at Catholic Answers
Author of *Why We're Catholic*

"I loved *Rekindled*—it is quick, concise, and super transparent. Mallory Smyth's honesty is a gift to so many Christians and Catholics alike and *Rekindled* is an essential read for parents of adult children who have left the faith or have become lapsed in their practice. This book belongs in every Catholic home."

Jenny Uebbing
Blogger at *Mama Needs Coffee*
Creator and content director of Off the Charts

"At a time when so many young people are confused and searching for moral clarity, Mallory Smyth's story of coming back to the Catholic faith, *Rekindled*, demonstrates the power of the Catholic Church to give young people what they need."

Emily Stimpson Chapman
Creator of *The Catholic Table* blog and
coauthor of *The Catholic Almanac*

Rekindled

How Jesus Called Me Back to the Catholic Church and Set My Heart on Fire

Mallory Smyth

AVE MARIA PRESS AVE Notre Dame, Indiana

Founded in 1865, Ave Maria Press is a ministry of the United States Province of Holy Cross.

www.avemariapress.com

Paperback: ISBN-13 978-1-64680-009-4

E-book: ISBN-13 978-1-64680-010-0

Cover image © tobi/Getty Images.

Cover and text design by Brianna Dombo.

Printed and bound in the United States of America.

Library of Congress Cataloging-in-Publication Data
Names: Smyth, Mallory, author.
Title: Rekindled : how Jesus called me back to the Catholic church and set my heart on fire / Mallory Smyth.
Description: Notre Dame, Indiana : Ave Maria Press, 2020. | "Smyth editorial final." | Summary: "In Rekindled, Smyth traces the story of her own disillusionment and departure from the Catholic Church followed by a rediscovery of the beauty and truth of Catholicism. This book illuminates the reality of a Church that is both holy and in need of perfection"-- Provided by publisher.
Identifiers: LCCN 2020028869 (print) | LCCN 2020028870 (ebook) | ISBN 9781646800094 (paperback) | ISBN 9781646800094 (ebook)
Subjects: LCSH: Smyth, Mallory. | Catholics--Biography. | Ex-church members--Catholic Church--Biography.
Classification: LCC BX4705.S6633 A3 2020 (print) | LCC BX4705.S6633 (ebook) | DDC 282.092 [B]--dc23
LC record available at https://lccn.loc.gov/2020028869
LC ebook record available at https://lccn.loc.gov/2020028870

To every person I ever called "friend," I wrote this with you in mind. No matter where you are in your life, my prayer is that you will fall in love with the God who loved you first and find the Truth that he offers. He came that you would have life to the fullest!

To my parents,
who always encouraged me to revisit Catholicism throughout all my searching.

Contents

Introduction **

This will be the ninth year that I have been working in full-time Catholic ministry. It's been almost a decade since I called my parents and told them that I was quitting my promising career in accounting so that I could live on half that salary as a local youth minister. Every parent's dream, right? I'll never forget that conversation, mainly because my parents were furious, but also because I lied about the pay cut I was taking in an attempt to soften the blow. I was going from making somewhere in the fifty thousand dollar range to making twenty-nine thousand in my ministry job. I told my dad that it was thirty-one thousand because I thought the thirties sounded better. (Don't worry; I confessed the lie to a priest pretty quickly and to my dad years later.)

Despite the rocky start to my work in the Church, it's since been an incredible nine years. I have worked in youth ministry, as a FOCUS missionary, and in women's ministry with ENDOW and Walking with Purpose. I have seen hundreds of people of all ages discover what it means to be Catholic. I have seen what happens when the light bulb of true faith comes on and people realize they can have a living relationship with God. I have seen men and women enter religious life who give me great hope for the next fifty years of Catholicism. Revival is happening everywhere, and it is the honor of my life to witness it unfold.

Mixed with these joys, however, are some deep sorrows. If you have ever read the statistics on Catholic Church attrition, you know they aren't good. Millions of men and women have left the Church for a myriad of other belief systems, or none at all. I have met fallen-away Catholics so often that I can pick them out by their response when I tell them what I do. I can almost tell a version of their story before they begin to tell it to me. I know them not only because I have sat with so many of them but also because I was one of them. Years before I made that phone call to my parents, I had one foot out of the Catholic Church and the other was soon to follow. And like the stories of so many disillusioned Catholics that I have heard, my story too starts with the simple phrase "I was raised Catholic . . ."

My parents are from large Catholic families, and since I am from south Louisiana, I honestly grew up thinking that everyone had fifty cousins, celebrated Mardi Gras, owned a boat, and was Catholic. As a kid, Catholicism showed up in every part of my life because Catholicism permeated our Cajun culture. I attended an above-average Catholic elementary school, we prayed the Rosary often as a family, and my parents talked about God on more than just Sundays. I had a positive relationship with religion and naturally gravitated toward faith until other things became more important.

As I went into middle school, my religiosity started to take a back seat to my social life, and I noticed the same pattern in my friends. Who wants to worry about "God" and "prayer" when boys and friend drama require so much attention? This could have been the end of the road for me and any sort of meaningful Christianity, as it was for many of my classmates, if it weren't for my brother making his Confirmation. He experienced a deep conversion on his Confirmation retreat, and I saw for the first time in my life what it looks like when a young person gives his life to Jesus. I learned through my brother that Catholicism is more than just a religion: it is a relationship with God. I learned that Jesus loved me and wanted me to be good, so that is exactly what I decided to do. I joined my church youth group, where I met faith-filled adult leaders whose lives were shining examples of Christianity lived out. I prayed, read scripture, joined a Bible study, and went to daily Mass at my high school. Over time, I became known as the "good Christian girl," and I was good at being good—until I wasn't.

During my junior year, I got my first boyfriend, and within a year the faith that I thought was so strong had crumbled as the glamour of secular culture beckoned and life got complicated. Leaving high school, I was slightly more "religious" than anyone else, and three shifts occurred in my thinking.

The first shift came from the effects of giving in to temptation. As a Catholic, I knew about forgiveness and the love of God, but I learned that only after I learned to follow the rules. I learned all the dos and don'ts of morality and, oh yeah, Jesus loves you. But what about when I no longer followed the rules? What about the times that I had given into temptation and become a hypocrite? Was I a Christian then? Was I worthy of standing in front of the Almighty? As my choices changed, I started to feel like a liar—unworthy of God's goodness and the "good Christian girl" reputation I had earned.

The second major shift occurred when the lifestyles of those I loved most started to clash with the seemingly antiquated teachings of the Church. I was in theater, and many of my male friends were gay. I worried what the Church said about them because, in my opinion, they were pretty awesome. And what about my promiscuous friends? They didn't seem to be living the gloom and doom promised to us in religion class. In my daily experience, it seemed that one could pretty easily step out of the bounds of Catholic Church teaching and not end up in ruins.

The last major shift was that faith no longer seemed relevant in my everyday life. For years, my Catholic faith was important, but I never developed an integrated, Catholic understanding of reality. There was God and what he wanted from me on one side, while my dreams of success, friendship, and lifestyle were on the other. They rarely mixed. Walking into my freshman year at Louisiana State University (LSU), I chose to give more attention to my idea of happiness, and I put anything having to do with religion on the back burner.

For the next three years, my life looked like that of your average state school college student. I joined a sorority, studied just enough to get decent grades and not screw up my future, and partied a few times a week (not too much to get a reputation, but just enough to be known as "fun"). I spent most Sundays, especially during football season, hungover on the couch somewhat pleased with my weekend but vaguely aware that I was far from the woman I was meant to be. I went to church about half the time and only to appease the demands of my background as the embers of faith in my heart continued to cool.

During the summer of my junior year, I was getting ready to meet my friends at the bar for a low-key night of drinks. I was twenty-one, so I wasn't necessarily doing anything wrong, but something felt different. As I stood in front of the mirror, doing my makeup, my heart sank. I did not want to go. I stared at myself and saw that I was exhausted by my life of self-indulgence. I no longer had the naive spark of joy I'd once had. Over the past three years, in my efforts to live a "normal" American college lifestyle, free from the confines of religion, I had done things that now made me wince. This freedom I sought had come at the price of my self-respect. My lack of confidence was, in many ways, an honest assessment of my lifestyle. I didn't like what my life was starting to look like, and I knew I would not achieve my dreams of happiness, success, and true love by sipping a Crown and Coke at the local LSU dive bar.

I knew that I had been much happier when I was living my life as a Christian, but the problem was that I no longer really believed in God. I behaved as though there were no God, and in the end, that behavior became my belief. I decided that night that something had to change, and I would start that change by exploring what it would look like to live the life of an atheist.

The next week, I went to Barnes & Noble to purchase *The God Delusion* by Richard Dawkins. I knew that he was brilliant, and I expected to find the answer I was looking for in the pages of his book. I suspected that a life of moral atheism would be the life for me and that my still-believing family would have to respect that.

I was wrong.

I read the book from cover to cover, and despite my hopes, I found myself right back on the edge of belief—at the beginning of the road I had walked years ago. Reading the book, I realized that I didn't fit into any of the categories of people who "needed" religion. I didn't look to religion for comfort or for a reason to behave, and I wasn't uncomfortable with the idea that there may be nothing after death. I was much more interested in finding the truth, whether I was comfortable with that truth or not.

By the end of the book, I finally had to admit that I am just not smart enough to disprove the consensus of all of human history. Dawkins mentioned that every group of people in history has believed in a creator. People far more accomplished and virtuous than I knew God who existed before creation. What did I, with my 3.2 GPA at a state school, have to say to them? How could I unequivocally disprove what many of them had proven? They may have had access to less information than I, but these philosophers, theologians, and saints blew me out of the water when it came to wisdom and virtue. If they could give their lives to God, then I could, at the very least, say a prayer. I sincerely looked at the ceiling and said, "Lord, I don't know if you are real, but I am jumping on your team, and you better prove yourself to me." And over the next few years, he did just that.

The problem was, I had no idea just how I was going to go about "jumping on God's team." I mean, how does one even begin to shift belief and attitude and behavior? I had a lot of work to do, and I wasn't sure how to bring my childhood faith into my young adult life. I thought of my Christian sorority sisters. I was friendly with them but had always politely turned down their consistent invitations to their nondenominational church. With nowhere else to go, I decided I would start there. I had spent little time in the Protestant church, but I didn't like the Catholic church on campus, and I knew that I wouldn't be alone if I went with my sorority sisters.

I was blown away by what I experienced the first night I attended a nondenominational worship service. Walking in, I was welcomed by a stranger's warm smile, and everyone seemed friendly and eager for the service to begin—a far cry from the gloom of obligation present on the faces of most Catholic college students of the same age. I noticed a countdown approaching zero on the projector screen above the stage. I took my seat with hesitant excitement as the countdown finished and the band appeared on stage. They sang their opening praise and worship, and I watched the millennial congregants raise their hands in prayer. The music was good, really good. I had heard this kind of music at Catholic youth conferences but never during a regular Sunday service.

The praise and worship ended and out walked the thirty-something-year-old pastor in his jeans. You know the type—many are celebrities now—but at this time, I had never seen such an approachable pastor. And what followed, of course, was the part of the service that hooked me. The preacher opened the scriptures and brought them to life. I had heard wonderful preachers before, but I had never seen anyone preach with such knowledge of his subject, understanding of how to apply it to our lives, and passion for Jesus Christ. Sitting in my seat that night, I knew there was an entire world of Christianity that I had missed, and I wanted more. As the very cool band finished their closing song, I felt hope that I hadn't felt in years. I got in my car that night knowing that next week, I would be back. And I was.

Over the next year, I attended church every week. I even started lifting my hands unapologetically in worship. I finally realized that Jesus didn't want me if I was good enough; I could never be good enough. He wanted me as the train wreck that I was, and his love would restore me. I fell in love with Christianity, and with Jesus Christ. My behavior outside of church, however, still often resembled my old life. I learned that it is easier to transform a heart than it is to transform a habit, but God was there in the midst of it. He had a plan, and that plan showed up in my life as a fiery, five-foot-tall Baptist girl named Andrea.

I met Andrea while I was working at the LSU Museum of Art, a place that required me to attempt the impossible task of being quiet at work. Andrea showed up with the only other animated personality in the place, and we became friends. I learned that her husband was the lead music pastor at the church I was attending. She was also chasing after holiness in a tenacious and frankly annoying way. She challenged me to clean up my behavior outside of Sunday church services with an audacity that I would have allowed from very few people, but she had the moral authority to do it. I remember a particular argument we had about drinking:

"Mallory, you can't get drunk."

"Andrea, I'm a Catholic from south Louisiana—it's what we do; you just don't understand."

After a bit of back and forth, the conversation ended. She won it fair and square a week later, when I woke up with a splitting headache knowing that the Lord wanted more for me.

During my time at the nondenominational church, through my close friendship with Andrea, the Lord transformed my life. That transformation was solidified forever when I went on a mission trip to Prague. I spent five weeks in that beautiful, once Catholic, and now primarily atheist city, learning how to pray daily and share my faith at a level that I had never before experienced. It was during my daily quiet times with the scriptures and in the moments when I just wanted to quit and go sightseeing that the Lord finally sealed my heart for good. I was his, not perfect but not going anywhere ever again. I had found the love of my life. I had found the truth, the purpose, the joy, and the meaning for which I had longed. I knew that I had to be about God and his Church no matter what, and I had found it outside of the folds of Catholicism.

For three years, I stayed away from the Catholic Church as my bitterness toward the faith of my youth grew. How had I been in Catholic schools for twelve years but never received a comprehensive, Gospel-centered worldview? As Jeff Cavins, a well-known Catholic Bible teacher would say, I received "a pile of Catholicism." While my pile made more sense than those of my far less catechized peers, it still wasn't enough. In the first twenty years of my life, I had only heard preaching with deep conviction a handful of times, and I had heard well-rehearsed, pleasant worship music much less than that. I knew only ten or so Catholic adults in my life who had made Jesus the center of their lives. These ten men and women had a profound effect on me, but most of the adults I knew attended Mass, and that was it. The other parts of their lives were spent in pursuit of material pleasures and making moral compromises, just as mine had been. It was as if when I spoke to my Catholic friends, most of whom were no longer practicing, we weren't even talking about the same God or even the same Christianity. Everything in me wanted to live a life centered on the Gospel of Jesus Christ—and nothing about that desire said "Catholic" to me.

This is how I felt as a twenty-four-year-old. I didn't want to be Catholic. I had graduated college, started a job in Tampa, and gotten involved with a Protestant church there. I was still loving being a non-Catholic Christian, and yet there was something, a remnant in my heart causing me to question if I could really leave Catholicism forever. Call it family ties or good old Catholic guilt, but in the end, I know it was the working of the Holy Spirit. Out of nowhere, on a random weeknight, I found myself pulling into my local Catholic church to attend eucharistic adoration.

I sat there in the pew that night completely familiar with what I hadn't seen in years. I had been to adoration many times in my life, but not since I stopped doing the Catholic thing. That evening, the Lord worked his magic. The priest was friendly and joyful. He seemed genuinely holy, something that I saw as rare at the time. As I stared at the Eucharist that night, I knew in my heart what I had known forever. Before me was the Jesus with whom I had fallen so in love. It was him. I remembered the teachings that Eucharist is the Body, Blood, Soul, and Divinity of Jesus Christ, and I believed it.

In my car that night I pleaded, "Lord, what do you want from me? I would go anywhere for you, but I can't be Protestant and Catholic; I have to choose." I know that God doesn't always answer prayers audibly, but that night, I heard him loud and clear: "I have raised you in this Church. Many of my people no longer know me. I have given you a mission field. Why are you searching for another one?" In that instant, out of obedience, I decided that I would stay and make my home in the Catholic Church.

After that night, I mostly stopped going to my Protestant activities. I kept my Protestant friends and occasionally joined Bible studies, but I gave most of my attention to the Catholic Church. I started, reluctantly, to attend Mass weekly, all the while complaining in my heart. Where was the thriving community I left? Still filled with pride, not desiring to understand the hearts of my Catholic peers, and very much wanting to make my parish "more Protestant," I started volunteering for the youth group.

During my time volunteering for youth ministry, I had no real love for the Church, but I knew I had to find answers. I decided that it was time to find the answers to my questions as I started typing them into the Google search bar. If I was going to be Catholic, I needed to know what the Catholic Church actually said about all of my questions. How do Catholics engage with Mary? Or predestination, the idea that God has already chosen who will be saved and we can do nothing about it? What does it mean to be Catholic and have gay friends? How does the Catholic Church make sense of sexuality? Where do Jesus, the Gospel, and evangelization fit into any of this? I knew the sound-bite answers to all of these things, but I needed to own the *whys* of Catholicism for myself.

I read the catechism clips, the scriptures, the blog posts, and the articles. By the end of it all, through my research, I had fallen in love with the Catholic faith. I realized I was wrong about most of my critiques. I learned that the Gospel of Jesus Christ is at the front and center of Catholicism. Catholics care about evangelization so much that we uphold our greatest evangelists as saints. The Catholic Church gave us the Bible in the first place and many ways to encounter it—daily in the Mass readings, in lectio divina, and in scriptural meditations that we can pray through to enable the Holy Spirit to speak to us. I learned about the dignity of the human person. I finally understood that the Church "has so many rules" because sin has real, tangible, life-destroying consequences. The Church's teachings on sexuality, marriage, and family are some of the most eye-opening teachings that I have ever read. Through my research, I learned what it meant to operate in reality as a Catholic. Finally, Catholicism merged with my reality in such a way that I could see the reality of Jesus Christ and his Church moving throughout history, into the present, and into my life. The story was making sense, and I saw how I fit in.

My dad had told me for years that the Catholic Church is the fullness of Truth, and I could finally see what he was saying. Everything that I loved about being Protestant existed to a greater and more glorious degree in the Catholic Church, right down to the Communion of Saints and the real presence of Jesus Christ in the Eucharist. In the Catholic Church, there is a deeper invitation to prayer, study, mission, and joy. It's all there, so why was the experience of it all so different from what I was learning? If these teachings are so amazing, so life changing, so Jesus-centric, then what the heck is going on in our religion classes, our Masses, and our Catholic institutions? Why had it taken me so long to discover the rich, mind-blowing, life-changing beauty of being Catholic? Why have so many Catholics lived their entire lives never even knowing that it's all there waiting for them?

This, my dear friend, is why I am writing this book. It is everything I would want to say to you if we were sitting on an airplane and you casually mentioned that you are a lapsed Catholic. For at least the past three generations, our everyday experience of Catholicism has done an incredible disservice to the faith that we profess and the people who are supposed to profess it. I have watched my generation bleed out of the Church, and since I was one of them, I don't blame them.

The Catholic Church contains within her deposit of faith the best news in the universe, but we have hidden it away with lousy catechesis, awkward experiences within the parish, and leadership that has failed to stay true to Jesus Christ and his Church, as well as our own personal proclivity toward sin and our tendency to turn away from the living God. There is a significant gap between the beauty that awaits us in the teachings of Catholicism and the lackluster daily experience of the average Catholic. This is what I seek to explore.

At face value, there are a million valid reasons to leave the Church for anywhere or anything else, whether it be the local Protestant church or atheism or yoga-type spirituality, and we who are living out the Catholic faith need to face this with boldness. There are also, hidden under the mess, infinite reasons to embrace Jesus Christ, his Church, and his mission. We must bring them to light. All of these reasons eventually boil down to one: Christianity is the Truth, and Catholicism is the fullness of that Truth. It is the answer to the desires of the human heart.

I hope for your sake that I can do justice to both. This is not a book that is meant to bash the Church, although I do not intend to sugarcoat any of the problems plaguing the Church today. I want to talk about them honestly, hopefully even with a sense of humor, as I believe that every Western Catholic alive will be able to relate to the issues in at least one if not all of the chapters. After discussing these issues, I hope to share with you what I learned about the Church and why I fell in love with being a Catholic. There is more than meets the eye here. While there is much work to be done, it would be a shame for those of us who were raised in the Church to miss the jewel that has been right in front of us all along.

1.
Going beyond Mediocre Masses

What I Experienced

My dear college friend Barton and I were catching up over iced coffee at a local trendy shop in Houston, Texas. I was one of the few LSU students who didn't immediately move to Houston after graduation, so I always have tons of friends to catch up with during my visits, and Barton is one of my favorites. He brings intelligence and wit to every conversation. We caught up on everything—what it's like living where we do, who we were dating, and the ups and downs of work. I told him stories from ministry, and he told me about his world of real estate development.

As our coffee time came to a close, the topic of Sunday plans came up. "Want to do brunch tomorrow?" he asked.

"I'd love to, but I'll be going to Mass in the morning."

"Oh great; I'll come too and then we can go to brunch."

"That sounds good; I'll give Heidi a call and invite her too." To my great surprise, my friend Heidi told me that she, too, would come for Mass and brunch. All of my friends from college, except for two, are no longer practicing Catholics. Normally, if I get too

1

"Jesus-y" on them, they kindly change the subject, and when it comes to my life of ministry, they take a "you do you" approach. Imagine my shock this Saturday when, by the time I had talked to everyone, I had four fallen-away Catholics ready to attend Mass with me. I knew how impactful one good Mass experience could be. I prayed and hoped that we would find a church service that would blow them away and bring them right back into the folds of faith.

We arrived the next morning at a parish in a wealthier part of Houston. We found a pew, and the cantor started the opening hymn with a pitch no one else could hit. In response, the congregation stood silently with blank faces. Churches often have bad music and uninterested participants, but this time it was different. I don't know if I just wanted it to be good for my friends and so I noticed it all so much more, or if was actually worse than usual. Either way, I knew they noticed too—a glaring reminder of why they don't normally do this.

As the Mass continued, I realized the poor singing and lack of participation were trivial compared to the attitude of the priest. Rarely in my life had I seen a priest so uninterested in the ritual at hand. Every move he made on that altar revealed how little he cared. There was no inflection in his voice. The homily communicated nothing, especially nothing about the Christian life, and by the way he handled Communion, you would think he was simply giving out stupid pieces of gum. Again, the congregation responded by receiving the Eucharist with blank faces, Louis Vuittons in hand, ready to complete their obligation and get the hell out of there. I understood. I had given my life to ministry for Jesus Christ and his Church, and even I could see how one's time would seemingly be better spent on literally anything else.

I sat there yelling at the priest in my mind. *I brought them to you! I brought them here to the table, to Jesus Christ himself! The least you could do is make them want to come back! The Mass is meant to bring forth the deepest mystery in the universe—can we at least do it a bit of justice? And why give your life to something you don't seem to believe anyway?* I wished I could actually say that to the priest so that I could hear his response. I wished that I could convince my friends that being a Catholic was the best thing ever, despite what this Mass showed them. I wished that they wanted what I had found, and I knew that at some level they did or they wouldn't have attended Mass that day. The Church had missed another opportunity for evangelization. I could say what I wanted to my friends, but their personal experience had a voice too. Walking out of the church that day, totally disheartened, I knew that my dear friends would not be returning, and I was right.

I would bet millions that you have had the similar lackluster experiences at Mass. You don't really want to go, but it's what your family does. You aren't quite sure what's happening or why you go in the first place. And let's face it: it doesn't really make a difference in your life anyway. After years of sitting, standing, and kneeling for no particular reason, it gets tiring. Every single Catholic in America has experienced the sometimes endearing but generally frustrating mediocrity of the Sunday service. Even if you happened to grow up in a wonderful, vibrant church with great community, good music, and great messages, I imagine that you were well aware that your parish was the exception, not the rule.

It's not just bad music. It's disengaged priests such as the one in Houston who either quit writing new homilies or gave sermons that managed to stir the soul with all the passion and excitement of waiting on dial-up internet. It's the ones who are so overzealous that every congregant walks out assured of their place waiting in hell. It's those crotchety people who have been in the pews for years harboring their judgment and refusing to move for the newcomer; these Catholics attend Mass every week but don't go out of their way to welcome anyone and don't seem as if they've ever met Jesus. Sometimes it feels as if they are actively trying to get people to leave the Church.

I remember my sister-in-law telling me of the time that a eucharistic minister refused to give my six-year-old nephew a blessing because it was "against the rules." Are you kidding me? We literally bless people when they sneeze. My brother and sister-in-law are committed Catholics for better or worse, but if they weren't, they could go to any one of the Protestant churches in the area and blessings would be bestowed upon them in abundance. There is one down the road from their house that actually specializes in making church awesome for little kids. The music is concert worthy. The preaching is powerful and relatable. Not only are they hospitable, but also they have an entire committee dedicated to hospitality. That's right: an entire group of people is intentionally strategizing on how to make you feel welcome on a Sunday. And if that isn't impressive enough, we cannot forget the coffee shop in the church. You can still worship with one hand up and your coffee in the other.

I went to one of these kinds of churches for years. Why wouldn't I? Why wouldn't you? It makes total sense that Catholics would stop going to a Mass that we don't understand and that feels like a time warp in all the worst ways. I hear the statistics that only 21 percent of professing Catholics attend Mass weekly,[1] and I get it. Out of many of my childhood friends who were raised Catholic, almost none of them still attend Mass or practice any part of Catholicism at all, along with millions of people around the world.

Faithful Catholics see the problem and are heartbroken, but so often I hear defenses of the Church only from those who have been won over by the beauty and truth of its teachings. After my time in the folds of great Sunday productions in the nondenominational services, I too was won over by the beauty and truth of Catholicism. I found that everything I loved about being Protestant was waiting for me in the Catholic Church to be discovered at a fuller, deeper level. Living my life as a devout Catholic has brought me deep, abiding joy, but I discovered these riches only after spending years away from my Catholic faith, first on the verge of atheism and then in other churches.

I am not saying that rock-star church services are what the Catholic Church needs in order to keep people in the pews or to facilitate the highest form of worship. I don't believe this, and I don't worship in this manner. I think we must, however, recognize that the laziness with which we have conducted and participated in the Mass for generations has made the rock-star church model attractive. We cannot ignore the many ways that those of us in the Church have failed the millions of men and women who are no longer in the pews. It is completely valid to stop participating in something that you don't understand and that doesn't bring you closer to God. If the Sunday experience, which is supposed to be the pinnacle of Christian worship, continually fails to capture your heart, I may long for your return, but I cannot blame you for leaving in the first place. For every good reason to leave, however, I have learned over the years that there are infinitely more reasons to stay. They are simply hidden, waiting to be found by those willing to look a bit deeper.

What I Learned

After spending a few years away from the Catholic Church, I made the decision that I would return to the Church of my youth. I had done so after prayer and out of obedience to God, but I had no deep affection for Catholic traditions or teachings.

During the summer I made this decision, my good friend Alberto had invited me to the New Orleans Museum of Art to see an exhibit showcasing Pope John Paul II's visit to New Orleans. I had many negative opinions about the Catholic Church, and I walked around the exhibit ready to judge anything at any moment. This day, I would reflect later, marked the beginning of the undoing of my complaints and misunderstandings about the Church's teachings and intentions.

We got headphones that gave us audio commentary on the exhibition, and as we wandered through the halls of the museum I saw the "usual Catholic stuff" such as priest outfits, crosses, and pictures of Pope John Paul II with Mother Teresa. I turned the corner into an exhibit room and saw a gigantic monstrance enclosed in glass. A monstrance is a holder for the Eucharist, and this one looked as if it were fit for a king. It was pure gold with precious jewels all over it.

I started to feel indignant. *The money of the Catholic Church*, I thought. *Why does that monstrance have to be so outrageous when a simple, smaller one would work just fine? It's all so extravagant when so many people are in need.* The recording in my headphones then started to explain the story of this precious instrument, and my pride got a punch in the gut.

The monstrance was created for the 1938 Eucharistic Congress of the Diocese of South Louisiana, which at the time was New Orleans and everything below it. (If you think that it's only ocean, you would be wrong!) In order to create a holding place for the Eucharist at the congress, the archdiocese sent out letters to all the Catholics asking for personal donations of old jewelry so that a proper holding place could be made for the Body of Christ. The response was overwhelming. Thousands of people sent in not only their old jewelry but also their most prized possessions. The faithful donated their wedding rings, their precious metals, and their rare gems. The diocese then melted down these beautiful gifts and made a magnificent monstrance, one fit for a king, to hold the Blessed Sacrament.

I was in tears. I started to understand that all of the grandeur had a purpose. All of those obnoxiously ornate "Church things" were the result of extravagant acts of love made by people to honor their God, with the same spirit as the woman who anointed Jesus' feet with expensive oil. They were a gift to God in time and a gift to us through time. How lovely it is that anyone, no matter their social status, can stand before a monstrance or a tabernacle or a cathedral and experience a beauty that can lift their soul to heaven. I had so much to learn about the intentions and history of the Church despite what I thought I knew. I realized I needed to ask questions with humility.

I was mostly, however, in awe of the generosity of so many people. This monstrance was an act of worship from ordinary people to their extraordinary God. It was the 1930s, in the midst of the Great Depression, that these men and women were giving away their precious possessions. What an incredible sacrifice.

Could you imagine something like that happening today? What if a diocese sent out the same letter for the same purpose? Our outrage culture would eat that for breakfast and then break the internet. "How dare they?" we would say. "The Church has enough money." That sort of large-scale generosity doesn't seem to exist anymore. These 1930s Catholics must have known something that we don't. They must have had a deeper understanding of this mystery that we call Catholicism to participate in this request so generously. So what did they know?

The Gospel

I truly fell in love with God in the Protestant church. It was there that I finally came to terms with the Gospel message. I'm sure you know at least some of it. *God is love. Jesus died for our sins.* I had heard these statements and even believed them for most of my life, but the gravity of it all never truly hit me until I was twenty-two. Someone in the Protestant church (I don't remember who) intentionally walked me through the Gospel, and it was as if I was hearing it all for the first time.

They began with the bad news: "All have sinned and fall short of the glory of God" (Rom 3:23). *Bad news?* I remember thinking, *this is great news.* If everyone has fallen short of the glory of God, if each one of us has gone our own way, then we are all starting from the same place. This truth set me free. I could stop trying to be better than other people. In reality, I was no better than them anyway.

Because we have fallen short of God's glory, because every single one of us has chosen creation over the creator, none of us deserve to be in the presence of God, and there is nothing we can do to actually earn our place in heaven. In our brokenness, there is no action we can take that can make us worthy of a perfect God. We cannot work our way to God's level of goodness. He, instead, in his perfection came to us. My good works can never make me worthy of God's love. It is God's goodness that claims me as worthy by the gift of Jesus' sacrifice on the Cross.

Maybe you have heard these statements before, but they've gone in one ear and out the other. We all know that Jesus died for our sins, but so what? Most of us don't even believe in sin, so how can we understand what it means for someone else to die for our sins? In order for me to understand the depth of love of Jesus' sacrifice, I had to come to terms with my own sin.

I could see the consequences of the darkness in my heart. I started to recognize my selfishness, my pride, and my desire to do things my own way, and for the first time, I understood that my actions had real consequences. When I acted in accord with the will of God, such as choosing to be selfless or honest when it didn't serve me to do so, there was a consequence of life. I built trust and goodness into a relationship and elevated my own character in the process. On the other hand, when I acted against God's will, there was always a death. If I lied to a friend, even if they never found out, that relationship now had a break in it for good and my character was degraded. I could see these life-and-death consequences in everything. The weight of this, the realization that I really am broken, unable to fix myself, changed everything.

For the first time in years, I stopped trying to white-knuckle my way into being a "good person." There is a great deal of talk in our culture about being a good person. We might say "religion exists to make us good people," or "as long as you are a good person, what does it matter if you aren't going to church?" The Gospel message makes us ask: Am I good compared to whom? To other broken people? In that case, all we have to do is find someone who likes the same sins we do and then we feel good about ourselves. Jesus said, "You, therefore, must be perfect, as your heavenly Father is perfect" (Mt 5:48). Are we good compared to our holy God? No. In that comparison, we are always found wanting.

I stopped trying to become an arbitrarily good person, and I started praying through the realization of what Jesus did for me. In my darkness, heaven was unreachable. In Christ, I was gifted heaven and the only appropriate response was gratitude, joy, and worship. Free from trying to be "good" on my own, I was free through the grace of Jesus Christ to pursue virtue with tenacity. Instead of fighting my way through, I started to fall in love with goodness as I could see that a life of freedom reflected the will of God.

It was through truly learning and understanding the Gospel that I first fell in love with the Lord and slowly started to devote my time to the very cool, local, nondenominational church. When my brother, a staunch Catholic, found out, he was angry. I will never forget getting into a yelling match over my car's Bluetooth with him because of this development.

I was going on a Protestant mission trip, taking a major step in my faith, and he was distraught that it wasn't a Catholic mission trip. At this time, I had tons of questions about Catholicism and so I said, "What does it matter, if I am bringing people to Jesus? Catholics aren't even very nice." I didn't understand why Catholicism or the Mass was important, and I was living out my faith way more than I had been six months prior.

He responded, "Mallory, if you don't bring people to love the Eucharist, you are only bringing them halfway." At the time, I saw him as a closed-minded jerk, but he was right. I didn't understand the Eucharist at the time or the incredible gift that God has given us in his presence in his Body and Blood. Years later, I sat listening to a homily as I toyed with the idea of committing myself fully to the Catholic Church, and I was humbled. I would never admit it to my brother, but I slowly started to understand what he was saying.

The Eucharist

The priest in Mass that day was preaching from the sixth chapter of the Gospel of John. If you have received poor Catholic teaching, and most of us have, you may not know that in this chapter you can find what theologians call the "Bread of Life Discourse."

The priest opened up his sermon with the image of Jesus teaching to a large crowd of his disciples. These men were asking for a sign that Jesus is the one from heaven. They say, "Our fathers ate the manna in the wilderness; as it is written, 'He gave them bread from heaven to eat'" (Jn 6:31). Jesus replies that it is his Father who gives true bread from heaven. "For the bread of God is that which comes down from heaven, and gives life to the world" (33). Jesus then says, "I am the bread of life; he who comes to me shall not hunger, and he who believes in me shall never thirst" (35).

The priest explained that at first glance, Jesus seems to be speaking in a metaphor. This is a common element of Jesus' preaching, as he compares himself to almost everything on the planet to get his point across. Here, however, I learned that he's speaking literally. The Jews, not understanding Jesus, start asking questions: "Is not this Jesus, the son of Joseph, whose father and mother we know? How does he now say, 'I have come down from heaven'?" (Jn 6:42). Jesus then goes all in: "I am the living bread which came down from heaven; if any one eats of this bread, he will live for ever; and the bread which I shall give for the life of the world is my flesh" (51).

Not surprisingly, the crowd does not like this at all, and they start grumbling and questioning. Continuing to paint the picture, the priest pointed out to us that Jesus does not take anything back but rather doubles down on his claim.

> Truly, truly, I say to you, unless you eat the flesh of the Son of man and drink his blood, you have no life in you; he who eats my flesh and drinks my blood has eternal life, and I will raise him up at the last day. For my flesh is food indeed, and my blood is drink indeed. He who eats my flesh and drinks my blood abides in me, and I in him. As the living Father sent me, and I live because of the Father, so he who eats me will live because of me. This is the bread which came down from heaven, not such as the fathers ate and died; he who eats this bread will live forever. (Jn 6:53–58)

Most of Jesus' disciples leave at this point. In the midst of the mass exodus, with emotions high, Jesus turns to the apostles and asks them if they want to leave. Peter responds, "Lord, to whom shall we go? You have the words of eternal life; and we believed, and have come to know, that you are the Holy One of God." (Jn 6:68–69).

The priest that day completed his homily by explaining that this is Jesus' longest continual discourse on any given subject throughout all of the gospels and he was willing to lose his disciples—even his apostles—over it. I had never heard this narrative explained in such a connected way. I had never heard the Eucharist explained from the voice of Jesus in the scriptures. Sitting in the pew that day, it was easy for me to see that Jesus was clearly giving his followers more than a symbol of himself. He was giving them all of himself, in the flesh, for all of time.

Andy Stanley, a wonderful Protestant pastor, often tells his congregation that he is not a Christian simply because the Bible tells him so. He believes in Jesus because he rose from the dead, and since no one else has ever done that, whatever Jesus says goes. Peter was exactly right in what he said to Jesus. How can Jesus give his flesh for the life of the world? What can we even make of that with our human senses? What of the idea that God would give us his flesh in the form of bread so that he could literally become one with us? Can we handle it? It's an unworldly teaching from a man not from this world and from a God who is much more humble than his creation.

That day, I started to fall in love with the Eucharist. I finally understood what my brother had been telling me. Yes, we can bring people into a personal, transformative, vibrant relationship with Jesus through the Holy Spirit, and we should. In fact, most of our trouble stems from the fact that we have taught people how to be "Catholic" in practice but have failed to teach them how and why they should love Jesus. That personal relationship with Jesus, however, was meant for more than intimacy of spirits. It was meant for total intimacy of body and soul. He desires to be one with us, physically and spiritually, and he accomplishes that by giving us his flesh as true food and his blood as true drink.

The Catholic faith is the only faith that still believes that Jesus is present, Body, Blood, Soul, and Divinity, in the Eucharist. As I started to study the history of Christendom, I realized that all early Christians agreed on this. Even Martin Luther, the father of the Reformation, believed in the real presence of Jesus Christ in the Eucharist. He writes,

> Who, but the devil, has granted such license of wresting the words of the holy Scripture? Who ever read in the Scriptures, that my body is the same as the sign of my body? or, that is, is the same as it signifies? What language in the world ever spoke so? It is only then the devil, that imposes upon us by these fanatical men. Not one of the Fathers of the Church, though so numerous, ever spoke as the Sacramentarians: not one of them ever said, It is only bread and wine; or, the body and blood of Christ is not there present."[2]

It wasn't until the Protestant Reformation was well underway that the teaching was disputed and eventually left behind by most of Christianity.

If you are anything like me, you grew up receiving the Body of Christ every single week. I used to get in line as if to receive my token for going to Mass, completely unaware of what I was actually doing. It was my countdown to leaving. I had no idea that every time we take Communion, we are experiencing one of the deepest miracles in the universe. God became a man to save us. Yes, this happened once in time, but he continues to give himself to us over and over again at every Mass because he wants to be united with each one of us personally. I know how ordinary it can feel. There are many days that I walk up to Communion with my mind a million miles away—but that doesn't change God's faithfulness. My uncle, when speaking of the Eucharist, once said, "I don't remember every meal that I have ever had, but I know that every single one of them sustained me." Just because it seems ordinary doesn't change its reality.

Learning about Jesus, the Bread of Life Discourse, the writings of the saints of old such as St. Ignatius of Antioch who passionately defended the Real Presence,[3] and the fact that the father of the Reformation himself held an unwavering belief in the Eucharist gave me a new understanding of the Mass. If Jesus Christ makes himself present at every Mass, just so he can become one with me, then I can find it in myself to show up to receive my Savior into my hands and then into my being. As one of those people who have fallen so far short of the glory of God, I need a God who can come to me. I need a God who is able to pay for my sins, and I need a God who makes himself available to me in his entirety. This is our God in the Incarnation, in his Passion, and in the Eucharist. Only this kind of love can sustain the human race.

The Mass

But what of the Mass itself—why is it the way it is? Why the vestments, the piety, and the rules? You know, Catholics have a reputation for being obsessed with following the rules. The Mass as a worship service was something that I understood very little about before I returned to the Church. Only a few months ago, I was on the phone with a friend who no longer practices her faith and she mentioned that she was told we go to Mass because, "well, we are supposed to." That doesn't sound like a good reason to me. So, why the Mass? Why does it matter?

In my husband's and my room hang two pictures from the 1890s, one of the Sacred Heart of Jesus and the other of the Immaculate Heart of Mary. Oh, how I want to jump on the Joanna Gaines bandwagon with her shiplap and her farmhouse chic, but I could never do it. I'd rather my home look like a classy antique shop because, at the end of the day, I desire to connect to the past.

Old items and traditions root our souls to the human experience. It is in our nature to desire connection to something bigger than ourselves. This lets us make sense of our identity because we see how we fit into the big picture of life.

As a young Catholic, I knew little about the Mass. I knew that we participate in the Liturgy of the Word, the Offertory (or as I typically engaged with it, "intermission"), and then finally, the Liturgy of the Eucharist. I had no idea, however, that this hour-long, often-inconvenient ritual has been used by Christians to enter into deep, heavenly worship since the founding of Christianity. As I started to look into the teachings of Catholicism, I came across the words of St. Justin Martyr from about AD 155:

> On the day we call the day of the sun, all who dwell in the city or country gather in the same place. The memoirs of the apostles and the writings of the prophets are read, as much as time permits. When the reader has finished, he who presides over those gathered admonishes and challenges them to imitate these beautiful things. Then we all rise together and offer prayers for ourselves . . . and for all others, wherever they may be, so that we may be found righteous by our life and actions, and faithful to the commandments, so as to obtain eternal salvation. When the prayers are concluded we exchange the kiss. Then someone brings bread and a cup of water and wine mixed together to him who presides over the brethren. He takes them and offers praise and glory to the Father of the universe, through the name of the Son and of the Holy Spirit and for a considerable time he

gives thanks (in Greek: *eucharistian*) that we have been
judged worthy of these gifts. When he has concluded
the prayers and thanksgivings, all present give voice to
an acclamation by saying: "Amen." When he who pre-
sides has given thanks and the people have responded,
those whom we call deacons give to those present the
"eucharisted" bread, wine and water and take them to
those who are absent.[4]

This liturgy sounds a lot like my usual Sunday Mass, and this ritual
was referenced a little more than a hundred years after Christ's
death. The stories of Jesus in the early second century would have
been as fresh as the stories of my great-grandfather are today. It was
out of stories just like this that early Christian rituals were formed,
and the Mass has survived until today remarkably unchanged.
When I attend Mass, I am connected to every single martyr around
the world. I am participating in the worship of St. Augustine and St.
Thomas Aquinas; in the Mass, we are united with the Communion
of Saints throughout all of history.

Millennials and members of Generation Z often complain of
feeling aimless, disconnected from a solid foundation. In fact, much
of our behavior is driven by our desire to be part of something that
will last. In a podcast interview, R.R. Reno, editor of *First Things*,
remarked on the amount of tattoos that can be seen on millennials.
In a world where nothing stays the same, tattoos are a signal of the
desire for something solid and permanent.[5] If Jesus is truly present
in the Eucharist (as we have already discussed) and the ritual of the
Mass has been conducted for two thousand years, it would be hard
to find something more solid. Think about it: Until the Reformation, every Christian would have participated in the Mass in order
to worship God. Every person who reached the heights of holiness
to the point that we have given them the title "saint" would have
worshipped the Lord in the Mass. All the crooked, broken men and
women who were simply trying to understand God and make it
through this life would have participated in this same ritual. In the
Mass, we are taken out of our daily lives and are lifted to heaven.
Here we can become connected to this massive story that began

the moment God said, "Let there be light." Here, we can find our place in the story and find the face of our God.

As I continued to search for a deeper understanding of the Mass, I found much more than a mediocre, empty tradition. I found worship that overflowed with meaning, history, and majesty. My heart started soften, and then I learned what the Church actually says happens at Mass. It isn't just a physical act of worship committed by the people in the pews of a certain parish. The Mass is a mystical continuation of Jesus Christ's sacrifice on the Cross over all time and space. It's not a repeated sacrifice; rather, it's our continued participation in the one sacrifice of Jesus on the Cross.

Furthermore, the entire Church, past and present, angels and men, join in one accord to worship God altogether during the Mass. This means that every single Mass is a miracle in which the veil between heaven and earth is torn. When I attend Mass, no matter what I think of the externals, the realities are the same. Jesus Christ, the head of the ritual, is fully present—Body, Blood, Soul, and Divinity—in the Eucharist. The priest is standing in the person of Christ, and the congregation is uniting with all congregations on earth and all angels, saints, thrones, and principalities in heaven, glorifying God together. Honestly, my mind is blown as I write this. You may be wondering, *Is it true?* Well, millions of people who came before us believed it was true. Miracles occur during the Mass, and it seems that if true worship exists, it would resemble something incredible like that. With reasoned understanding, filled with the mystery of faith, I had to make the leap. I returned to Mass, determined to be a wholehearted participant regardless of my very many criticisms of how we humans mess it up.

So after years of knowing some of this in bits and pieces, not knowing how to put the puzzle together, I realized it was starting to make sense to me. I was made out of God's goodness, I rejected him in my sin, and he paid for the sin in his goodness. He was dead serious when he said, "For my flesh is food indeed, and my blood is drink indeed" (Jn 6:55). God didn't just incarnate himself for a certain people in a certain time. He remains with us to become one with us in the greatest miracle in history, and we can take part in that miracle at every Mass, the most ancient form of Christian worship in which all of creation unifies to glorify God. Further-more, our God is not so offended by crappy choirs and bad homilies that he refuses to show up. He is present in every celebration of the Mass because he is always faithful, even when we are not. Even when we are careless with the ritual or we mindlessly go through the motions, all of these glorious realities are there waiting for our participation.

Why I Stayed

When I was a missionary at the University of Tennessee, I expe-rienced what it is like when a southern state gets snow: everyone forgets how to drive. I was headed home from the Catholic center with my FOCUS missions teammate Andrea, and it took us an hour and a half to drive four miles. With little else to do, we decided to listen to a Lighthouse CD testimony of a woman named Anne Marie Schmidt.

Schmidt was a little girl in Czechoslovakia during World War II. As she described, she lived in an idyllic Catholic town, one in which she didn't even know the reality of divorce. During a Mass the Nazis invaded her town and brought countless horrors and atrocities. Schmidt's story is remarkable; truly, it was one miracle after another that continued to save her life. Of all the jaw-drop-ping details of her story, however, one incident that she mentioned stood out to me.

At one point, the Nazis rounded up the priests and one by one demanded that they renounce their faith. Schmidt stated that "the [priests] who attended daily Mass withstood the temptation, refusing to renounce their faith. It was the ones who didn't take the Eucharist regularly that caved."[6]

Stories like Schmidt's helped me realize that the Eucharist pro-vides enormous strength and grace, as if we were receiving God himself. If Jesus really is entirely present in the sacrament of the Eucharist, then the Catholic teachings on the Mass must be true. If this is how he wants to be worshipped, then who am I to choose a different way?

Is this the only way to connect with God? Of course not. God's presence is with us always, but he is with us differently, more intimately, in the Eucharist and in the Mass. We can worship the living God at any and every moment in our entire lives, but that worship takes on a new form for all of creation during the worship of the Mass.

For me, this means I have to go to Mass. If I know this, if I believe it, I must go to Mass. I need in my very being to worship. I need the sacrament that God offers to me in the most intimate of ways so that I can know him, be known by him, and then be transformed by him. I want to worship God in the way he wants to be worshipped, and so if he can handle the mess, then I can too.

With this attitude in mind, I have sat through some pretty bad services. I have gotten through Masses as far away from thinking of Jesus as the beaches of the Gulf Coast are from Colorado. But I have also wept through some of the most beautiful Masses in existence. I have sat in the pews, open to receiving from the Lord, and experienced a flood of grace. Most of the time, it has little to do with externals and everything to do with the disposition of my heart. I have gone from having an interest in God to rejecting him, desperately needing him, falling in love with him, and humbly worshipping him despite my unworthiness. I need to worship him because that is what I was made to do.

Yes, the human aspects of the Mass—from hospitality to music and community—need improvement. Many priests desperately need to increase their reverence for the Eucharist, their ability to preach a sermon that will inspire the audience, and their understanding of how to run a parish in such a way that is attractive, strategic, and financially sound. I implore and pray for those who are leading the Church to see what needs to be done and do it so that we stop bleeding out our people, but the one thing we don't need is a better sacrament or a better ritual. I implore and pray for those in the pews to get involved and "be the change they want to see." All of the mysteries are there for the taking, and we have an opportunity to do them justice.

So my friend, who for every good reason in the book no longer finds it worth your time to attend Mass, I want to tell you what

I hope for you every single Sunday that I sit in the pews. I hope you fall in love with God. I hope that you see yourself for exactly who you are in his eyes. Yes, fallen. Yes, broken. Yes, a mess. But loved—wholeheartedly loved—by the God of the universe. I hope that this Gospel message hits you like a ton of bricks and that you are met soberly with your need to worship well. Then I hope you will consider attending that often-mediocre Mass service that you attended when you were younger. I hope that you ask God to reveal himself to you in a way that assures you he is there and that he wants you there. He will be faithful to that request.

2.

Choosing More than Blissful *Ignorance

What I Experienced

C. S. Lewis's *Screwtape Letters* is a book written in the form of a series of letters between a senior demon, Screwtape, and his nephew demon, Wormwood. The letters reveal the advice that Screwtape gives to his nephew as Wormwood tries to woo his "patient," a human, along the path to hell. Throughout their conversation, Screwtape directs Wormwood to keep his patient from any real self-awareness at all costs. He tells him at one point, "Your business is to fix his attention on the stream of immediate sense experiences. Teach him to call it 'real life' and don't let him ask what he means by 'real.'" In keeping the patient distracted and from intentionally considering life's questions and what they mean for him, Screwtape tells Wormwood that his job will be much easier. He says,

> You will be gradually freed from the tiresome business of providing pleasures as temptations. As the uneasiness and his reluctance to face it cut him off more and more from all real happiness, and as habit renders the pleasures of vanity and excitement and flippancy at once less pleasant and harder to forgo (for that is what habit fortunately does to pleasure) you will find that anything or nothing is sufficient to attract his wandering attention. You no longer need a good book, which he really likes, to keep him from his prayers or his work, or his sleep; a column of advertisements from yesterday's paper will do. You can make him waste his time not only in conversation he enjoys with people whom he likes but in conversations with those he cares nothing about on subjects that bore him.[1]

This was the character of my life for many years. I watched hours upon hours of television when I was young. I spent most of my time in college consuming entertainment and taking part in shallow, useless living. But it was fun. All of my time was social, with little time spent on self-reflection or intentional learning. Yes, I was made for relationship with other humans, but I didn't understand that first and foremost, I was made for God. We are made to allow God to reveal not only himself to us but also ourselves to us. We were made to spend time reflecting, praying, and learning. There is a part of us that desperately needs this time to feel fulfilled. Distraction, however, is to us like water is to a fish. It's everywhere, and most of us spend so much time on distractions that we can't even see how it affects us. Most of us are not trained to be self-aware. The truth is there, but the comfort of our shallow pleasures keeps us from engaging.

During those years of total distraction, I can remember specific moments in which the Lord was explicitly trying to get my attention. I see places in my journey where Truth was trying to break through, and I just ignored them while chasing my version of happiness. The most vivid of these occurred when I was dancing to an eighties song at a bar filled with sweaty college students, shoulder to shoulder, drinking, dancing, flirting, and trying to find comfort in the opposite sex.

For a moment, I mentally stepped out of my buzz and surveyed the scene for exactly what it was. I thought to myself, *What if the lights went on and the music went off? What would I see?* I would see the truth of my surroundings. I was in a filthy warehouse, floors covered in cheap liquor, and young people desperate for self-esteem. If we turned on the light, the fun and the glam would be exposed for nothing more than a sham to make college students spend money on a night of regrets.

I remember thinking, *Is this it? Is this the pinnacle of this life? Is this the freedom I so yearned for during all those years waiting to leave my parents' house? How depressing.* For a split second, the truth grabbed me: this couldn't be the life for which I, or anyone else in the bar, was meant, and yet there we all were, in the same place, searching for the same thing. I had a choice. I could engage this realization and explore it more deeply, or I could ignore it and tell myself I would think about it later. I chose the latter.

For the next five years, I went back and forth between utterly distracted living and a deep longing for more. Overwhelmingly, the distraction won out. It was just too much effort to think differently or change my behavior. It wasn't until that moment, the one that I mentioned in the introduction when I was wearing the pretty blue dress, staring in the mirror, and getting ready to go to yet another bar, that my exhaustion won out. In another split second of self-awareness, I finally allowed myself to ponder life's questions with abandon. It became apparent that I needed to change.

Once I started to allow myself to ask the questions I had ignored for so long, I realized there is a whole world, a whole history, available to me. The most brilliant among us who have ever lived have spent their lives pursuing the answers to life's biggest questions. The pursuit of Truth puts everything in its place. Like turning on the lights in the middle of the bar, it reveals everything for exactly what it is. In this pursuit, you cannot help but start to see what has meaning and what doesn't. I began to realize that most of my searches were meaningless. What are status and material goods in light of eternity? They are nothing.

Years later, well into my journey with God, I was having an internet conversation with a dear friend of mine while we were both at work. We were talking way more than we should have been, but we were getting into a deep discussion on faith and belief. I finally asked her, "If you believe in God, and you know he would want you to live in a certain way, why don't you?"

"Mallory, I just don't care."

That was it. That was why I ignored God the many times he invited me into self-awareness that would lead to him, and why most of us believe in a higher power but do very little with that belief. We don't care. There is too much distraction, too many shiny things to pursue for us to desire to engage in really honest soul searching. We ignore the very questions that could lead us to a life of fulfillment because pleasure is everywhere. It is cheap and easy; it makes us feel good until it doesn't, and then there is another pleasure waiting to take its place. With the constant noise, distraction, and invitation of pleasure, most of us are not cultivating the type of inner life that would make us want to explore life's most profound questions.

The Church offers us a refuge from this noisy world so we can get to know ourselves and get to know our God. For many of us, silence is so scary and unnatural that we keep noise on at all costs. Whether it be TV in the background, binge watching the latest streaming series, video games, or music blasting in our headphones, we dare not be alone with our thoughts. The Church offers us such a gift, but we have not built ourselves into the type of people who can handle it.

For all the reasons to leave the Catholic Church, this one is on us. Most of us are too distracted to go deep. God offers us greatness, and we are too comfortable to become great. We see religion as outdated, old, and boring because its glory must be sought. To know God and live a life of fulfillment requires us to set ourselves aside and seek what will genuinely make us happy, and we need to embrace the wisdom, fortitude, discipline, and selflessness to do so. Sadly, all of these virtues are out of fashion.

What I Learned

It had been a few months since I left my promising career in accounting for all the glory of a Catholic youth minister's salary. I needed a side gig and had found one working party photo booths. It was a blast. Whether it was a wedding, a retirement party, or a party for no reason, the people were always really fun to talk to and the catered food was always delicious.

It was on our way to one of these parties that my fellow side-gig coworker and I were trying to get to know each other. As we drove, we covered every topic of small talk, testing each other for commonalities that might lead to friendship. We eventually landed on the topic of religion, and then my coworker told me that he was spiritual but not religious. "All religions have some truth in them, so how can we choose? We need to be good people." I had heard this thought process many times before and had even considered adopting it myself. "Spiritual not religious" people are likable because they don't make anyone mad. The problem for me is that I don't believe it. I know there is Truth, and there is not truth.

I looked at my coworker and said, "If Christianity claims to be the Truth to the exclusion of other religions and Islam makes completely different claims about Jesus than Christianity, how can they both be right? If half the world believes that God is real and the other half of the world doesn't believe in this God, how can these both be right? These are completely opposing beliefs, and the reality in which we live only has room for one. Someone has to be wrong."

His response was plain and simple: "You know," he said, "I'm not sure; I have never thought about that." Our conversation ended there.

My coworker had based his entire life's philosophy on something that he barely thought about at all. His life was comfortable, and his beliefs about life felt good. They made room for everyone, and they also gave him license to behave how he wanted. Why rock the boat?

Over the years, I have sat with hundreds of people of every age, people I know well, and people I don't know at all. Regardless of their generation, they tend to lean toward the view of my coworker. I often hear, "You know, I believe as long as you are a good person, that's what God wants," or "If you are finding your truth and you are happy, that's all that matters."

Only a couple years ago, I sat with my jaw on the floor as I was having dinner with one of my best friends. He and I had been very close when we were young but had lived different lives by the time we were in our twenties. He became an atheist, and I became a missionary. We sat on entirely opposing points of the political spectrum, and we would both disagree profoundly with certain aspects of each other's lifestyles. Contrary to popular belief, you can love someone with whom you disagree and enjoy spending time with them.

As we ate dinner, my friend told me about his work in the medical field, and so, of course, I shared about my life working for the Church. I was a bit uncomfortable, knowing that he doesn't believe in anything that I preach. To my surprise, he said to me kindly, "I think what you are doing is great. If you are giving people a message that makes them happy, then you are changing lives, and that's great." I was shocked. Here I am telling everyone that God exists, Jesus loves and died for them, heaven and hell exists, and people go there. My friend, who thinks that it is all nonsense, has no problem with me preaching a lie if it makes people happy.

I quickly responded, "Thanks, but if I have given my life to a lie, then I am not making people happy; I am deceiving them, and I desperately need to go work somewhere that pays me much more." We laughed a bit and then moved on to debate on whether a specific political candidate is a saint or the devil incarnate.

How did we get to a place where even the most intelligent among us are more interested in feeling good than finding Truth? Where did we lose our bold, tenacious search for answers to the questions that matter most in our lives? Why do we think we can fool ourselves into thinking that pleasure can substitute for genuine purpose or that platitudes about unity can bring us anywhere close to understanding reality?

One of the factors that has led us into the Jacuzzi of feel-good philosophy is that we live in the most prosperous time in human history. My husband and I often comment that on any given day, we, with our middle-class income, live better than the kings of old. Our homes may not literally be palaces, but more people than ever before have immediate access to almost any kind of food we like, temperature-controlled dwellings, and material goods sold at dirt-cheap prices. We also have direct, unbridled access to all the information in the world at our fingertips. "Spoiled" doesn't even begin to describe us. Now I know this is a generalization. Much of the world still lives in great, debilitating poverty, and we who have so much must respond to the needs of our brothers and sisters. It is overwhelmingly true, however, that if you live in the West, you are living better than someone of your status in the past. We no longer wake up every day and work to survive. Our basic survival needs are taken care of, for the most part.

So, we have ample time for leisure, which often turns into mindless consumption. Our focus on a greater good has become a focus on self-actualization, and we only ask big questions as they relate to us becoming healthier, wealthier, or more "fulfilled." Our big question is *How can we be more comfortable?* not *What is true?* Living like kings, we are not able to fight like warriors for the overarching good of humanity.

As we are more physically comfortable than we have ever been, we are also seeking more emotional comfort that we ever have. Archbishop Fulton Sheen said that humanity has lived through the age of faith and the age of reason, and we are now in the age of emotion.[2] We make decisions according to our feelings, which is the least honest of our faculties. We all know that following our "feelings" without engaging our will or our intellect has led us into disastrous situations. When we are basing our entire worldview on our emotions, we are bound to get it wrong because we can so easily miss Truth. In the age of emotion, we reject what makes us feel bad even if it is Truth, and we accept what makes us feel good, not caring if it is a lie that may lead us to destruction. The scriptures tell us in Jeremiah 17:9, "The heart is deceitful above all things, and desperately corrupt; who can understand it?"

Conversely, a common phrase in our modern culture is "follow your heart." Considering the statistics on loneliness and unhappiness, that mantra has gotten us nowhere. In the age of emotion, we perceive disagreement as an assault against our identity. We have lost the ability to admit that we might be wrong, for fear that our feelings may be hurt or our ego bruised. Our passions have led us away from a noble pursuit of Truth and rendered us too weak to correct our course.

The last reason we aren't seeking out truth and meaning (there are a million; these are only three) deals with a systematic downplay of Truth by the elites of society after World War II. Having been ravaged by two world wars in thirty years, society's elites feared the repercussions that could have occurred if such strong belief systems such as fascism and Nazism were to influence everyday citizens. To avoid this, they made it distinctly unpopular to hold any real view of absolute truth.[3]

These three factors have played a significant role in weakening our ability to seek the answer to life's most profound questions. There are a million other reasons as well, but we can't fool ourselves in the end. Years ago, I read a snarky article titled "7 Reasons the 21st Century Is Making You Miserable," and one of the reasons was that we can't fool ourselves into just having self-esteem. We are told to be confident, but we won't fool ourselves if we aren't doing anything about which we should be confident. We need to have some accomplishments under our belts to find that self-confidence, or it is all for show.[4] It is the same when it comes to meaning and fulfillment. We can't fool ourselves into shallow joy for long. Yes, momentarily, we can appease our souls, but it doesn't last. We end up with an ever-growing ache that will manifest itself in our lives in a host of unhealthy ways. This is where the God of the universe steps in, not as the one we can fashion into our trinket-y version of himself but as one who is the end to our ache. He demands of us what the world does not. He requires that we purify ourselves from the noise through silence, reflection, prayer, and a bold willingness to admit when we are wrong. He then soothes our ache and turns us into heroes.

When we skim along the surface of life, not caring what is underneath, the joke is on us. Jumping from pleasure to pleasure only leads us to emptiness as we become shadows of who God made us to be. Moral relativism is an opium that keeps us complacent, far from becoming heroes. When the drug wears off, however, we are still left with the ache. We were made for real Truth; we were made for a real and living God. In those small moments, we know we aren't fooling ourselves. We can either give ourselves over to more powerful, more soul-destroying distractions, or we can decide to take a different path.

Why I Stayed

As my reversion to Christianity deepened, I started making small changes in my life. I began to be more careful about the type of media I consumed. My life was still full of noise. I would study a verse in the Bible and then tune in to four back-to-back episodes of *Weeds*. I would belt out a Hillsong worship song in my car one minute and in the next work on memorizing Lil Wayne rap lyrics. My heart was shifting from an attraction to glamour to a yearning for God, but I had no silence in my life. If God was speaking to me, I couldn't hear him.

I only started participating in silence as a practice when I was obligated to on my mission trip to Prague after college. The mission team leaders informed us that we would be spending forty-five minutes to an hour in prayer alone, every day. I was excited for the opportunity to learn scripture, but I also didn't know what I would say to God for an hour every day. I mean, what could I possibly accomplish with so much quiet time? Wouldn't I run out of things to say?

As I sat in my breakfast nook with my Bible day after day, the Lord started to break through the barriers I had placed between us. He revealed to me my own heart. I had come such a long way, but the Lord revealed to me in prayer just how far I had to go. The Christian life is not about cleaning up behavior. It's about becoming like Christ. I had cleaned up much of my behavior, weeding out those big sins, but there was much more in my heart that the Lord wanted to reveal. The darkness wasn't the big stuff so much as the small, hidden deceits that directed me so subtly. He wanted to show me my grudges, my anger, and my jealousy because he wanted to deal with it. He wanted to show me just how deeply he loves me, regardless of this sin that had rooted itself in my heart while I was busy ignoring him for so many years.

As time went on, I continued to pray, and I started to build an inner life that could handle, even crave, silence. I developed an ear for the voice of God in my life. Most of us don't know the sound of the Lord's voice because we have crowded him out with a million other voices. The more I sat in the quiet, the more I yearned for it because I realized that silence is not empty. It is filled with the presence of God. In my prayer, I started to open myself up to the possibility of Truth, a Truth that I wasn't living. Years ago, I decided that I could be wrong and not be a bad person, and so I just let myself be wrong. Now, I allowed myself to become moldable in the hands of God.

This is precisely what happened with the human subject in *The Screwtape Letters*. In chapter 13, the patient starts to gain self-awareness by going on walks and reading books that he genuinely enjoys in the quiet. In a moment of silence, the patient decides to dedicate himself more deeply to God. Screwtape is very angry with Wormwood. In his amateur "demoning," he allowed his patient time to reflect, to ask deeper questions, and he found himself yearning for God. Screwtape angrily writes, "As a preliminary to detaching him from the Enemy, you wanted to detach him from himself, and had made some progress in doing so. Now, all that is undone."[5]

Screwtape revealed one of the secrets of the Christian life in this statement. Staying grounded in truth, beauty, and goodness will keep us connected to the source of it all, but for us to do that, we cannot give ourselves over to shallow living. We have to care about and pursue depth. What is the meaning of life? Why are we here? What is our overall and individual purpose? We owe it to ourselves to ask these questions and test the answers. One moment of reality can be all we need to bring us to our knees before God. One moment of honesty can shatter the glass that many of us have built around ourselves.

Friend, this is where the Church gets it right. Here, in the folds of its traditions, we find the heart of the Church. It offers us practices such as prayer, study, contemplation, and participation in the sacraments that lead us to a life of intimacy with God and self-knowledge. When we decide to pursue prayer and Truth within the movements of the Gospel, Catholicism offers us all that we desire. This is where the Church gets it right every time. It brings us to God through the ancient paths of prayer, study, and contemplation. When we are able to move beyond Catholicism's daily institutional shortcomings such as the poorly run Masses mentioned earlier, unfaithful priests, and widespread lack of formation, we can discover the best of the Church in its unadulterated, ancient doctrine.

The traditions of the Catholic Church introduce us to a life lived in communion with God and spent in pursuit of wisdom. There is no end to the wisdom offered us in the scriptures, the history of our Church, and the practice of living our faith daily. Intimacy with God is the foundation of everything else. It requires that we step away from the world and its noise. In silence, we start to get to know God in his nature and his character. He also reveals our hearts, the good and the bad, so that we can learn to sit with ourselves without feeling like we are drowning in our failings.

In studying the faith, as God has revealed himself in the Bible, and throughout the development of the Church, we start to gain wisdom. We can understand that there is nothing new under the sun. Everything has been tried before and will be tried again. Through the stories of the saints of old, we start to see our own stories and struggles. All the seeking in all the world always lands on one answer: God alone suffices. They who have God find they lack nothing. We can start to see the thread of sin and grace that connects us throughout time.

I stayed in the Church because, in this particular instance, it was I who was wrong. The Catholic faith was always right. Maybe you are like me, and you have had those brief moments of reality where you find yourself asking, "Is this all there is?" Maybe you have asked questions and didn't necessarily like the answers. Is it possible that you have allowed yourself to live in such distraction that you need to develop the ability to reflect in your life? Maybe you are asking all the right questions and are waiting for God to respond. He will. No matter where you are, I invite you to consider building up a life of silence, prayer, and study for yourself within the Catholic Church. You will be shocked by just how far you can go into the heart of our Lord and find the purpose he has waiting for you.

3.

Finding Real Answers to Good Questions

What I Experienced

"What are you doing?" a friend called across the quad.

"Dinosaur Gospel presentations," we yelled back. We got those looks that you get from strangers when you're doing something weird and everyone, including you, knows it. Dinosaur Gospel presentations are as silly as they sound, and yet the Holy Spirit can use anything to bring us to God.

It was my second year on staff with FOCUS, the Fellowship of Catholic University Students. In 2012, I became a missionary with FOCUS, which meant that I lived on a college campus, worked with a team of other missionaries, and served the college students in attendance by leading Bible studies and providing mentorship on how to live and share the Catholic faith. During my first year, I served at the University of Tennessee. I spent my second year leading a team of missionaries serving the students at Texas State University. It was here that the "dinosaur Gospel episode" unfolded.

On this particular day, Sarah, a college senior, and I were spending time together on campus talking to other students about religion. Since most students don't spend much time pondering eternal issues, they often welcome these discussions. Sarah and I, laughing at ourselves, grabbed dinosaur figurines as we headed to the quad. Our logic: Christianity can be intimidating, so let's make it less intimidating by humiliating ourselves. Brilliant, right? As we walked across the quad, a friend of ours spotted us from about twenty-five feet away. Her question, "What are you doing?" forced us to reveal ourselves to everyone within earshot. Our goal was to present the Gospel to people we had never met, using dinosaur toys.

As we shouted back to our friend, we heard a voice from behind us: "I'd like to see that." Sarah and I turned around to see a young man sitting on the quad's bobcat statue and interested in our silly antics. We walked over to him, introduced ourselves, made light conversation, and told him about the Gospel. We each used our dinosaurs, going back and forth, to explain that God created humanity out of his goodness, but humans chose creation over Creator and fell from grace. Humans can no longer get to God, and so God became a man to bridge the unbridgeable gap. It is in accepting and loving God that we can spend eternity with him.

He thought for a moment as Sarah and I stood in silent embarrassment. He was amused, maybe even impressed, but his face told me that he had questions. "Can you explain the mathematical possibility of Incarnation? It doesn't make mathematical sense." *Umm, what?* I can honestly say I have never received that question before or since. I had no idea what to say. This guy was much smarter than me, but heck, I know my faith, so I gave it my best shot. "Well, God is perfect. God is infinite. We are finite. When we sinned against God, we created an infinite problem. Since finite creatures cannot solve an infinite problem, infinity himself became finite to fix it." Boom.

To my shock, this answer was good enough for him. "No one has ever explained it like that," he said. "I went to the Catholic Church last year, looking for some serious answers. I received none, so I left and never came back." His words hit me like a bombshell. I was speechless. This young man had approached the Church on his own, searching for God and all he can reveal. He wanted Truth. He wanted something to soothe an internal ache, and he left empty-handed.

He even told me that he would have loved to come to our Catholic student social gathering if he hadn't already planned to drop acid that night. He hadn't found what he was looking for in the folds of Christianity, and so he settled for something else, somewhere else. I got his number and reached out to him, but we never reconnected.

I still think of that young man often. We, as the Body of Christ, should be noticing him and others like him who are genuinely searching. We owe them answers. I think of how I could have tried so much harder to connect with him again. I think of all the men and women, my friends and family, who grew up Catholic and still know nothing about Catholicism. It's not that they never asked; it's that they never received the real answers. This young man's story is not an exception. For millions of Catholics who have left the Church or who have nobly chosen blind faith, it's the rule.

I cannot tell you how many times someone has said to me that they asked their religion teacher a good and thoughtful question only to receive an answer of "It's a mystery," or "Just have faith." Just last week, my best friend told me that her teacher had told her about Mass on Sunday: "You don't go to be entertained; you go because you have to." How is this answer in any way winsome, convincing, or inspiring? My cousin asked his catechism teacher similar questions, genuinely wanting answers, and the teachers couldn't tell him anything that made sense. My cousin is one of the most naturally virtuous men I have ever met, and while he has a cultural interest in Catholicism, it holds very little weight in his life.

One of my Protestant friends married a Catholic, and so had to go through Catholic marriage preparation. Their marriage prep teacher told them they couldn't use birth control but couldn't give them any good answers regarding why the Church says no to artificial contraception, or how to go about family planning without it. My friend, drunk at his rehearsal dinner, told me all about this and said, "If your church can't give me a good alternative to birth control, then that's what we will use." I was about to burst but knew a rehearsal dinner is not the time to have an in-depth conversation about Natural Family Planning with the groom. If my Church couldn't give him answers, then he would find them somewhere else.

I can only bet that you have many of your own stories of you or your friends who had valid, honest questions about the faith. What proof is there that God exists? Why do bad things happen to good people? Why is there evil in the world if God is loving and kind? What is suffering? What sets Christianity apart from other religions? Yes, there is a point at which we do need to "just have faith," but Christianity is an intelligent faith in a God who has revealed himself. St. Paul tells us in Colossians 1:26 that "the mystery hidden for ages and generations [is] now made manifest to his saints."

God can be known, his ways can be searched, and his hand can be seen moving across the generations. Priests, monks, and sisters made many early scientific discoveries because they believed that God revealed himself to us in the universe, and so the more we understand the world, the more we can understand God. They found answers to the questions of creation by studying their faith, and they learned more about God by studying creation.

This is still true. God has revealed himself in the intricacies of ordinary life and the mysteries of theology. We can and should know both. We are meant to be able to give a reason for our hope (see 1 Pt 3:15). For too many years Catholics, in general, have been unable to provide those reasons.

Over the years, the lack of robust catechesis that has plagued our Catholic institutions has communicated to curious Catholics that there are no real answers. Is it surprising, then, that they conclude it is likely there are no answers at all? If the answers to life's most profound questions do not seem to exist in the Church, then it is no wonder so many have chosen not to stay.

What I Learned

Recently, I was watching two Catholic theologians discuss Catholic education, and one of the theologians compared our current situation to nutrition. He said that it is often the depletion of proper nutrition that is more dangerous to the body than the presence of toxins. If the body is deficient of nutrients, toxins can wreak havoc where they are able. On the other hand, if the body is properly nourished it is in a much better position to fight off pathogens that cause disease.[1]

This analogy described exactly what I had experienced in my own life and had seen in most of my peers' lives. Growing up in a faithful Catholic family, with decent Catholic schools and some good role models, I knew more about my faith than most, but it still wasn't very much. I did not receive a strong enough understanding of Catholicism to provide the right defenses against the opposing messages of the culture.

When I decided at the age of twenty-four that I would stay in the Catholic Church for good, I knew I had much to learn. I recognized different pieces of the Catholic puzzle but was unsure how they fit together. Seeking answers, I did what any millennial would do and turned to Google.

One by one, I researched my questions: What do Catholics actually believe about Mary? What do Catholics believe about the saints? What is the deal with Catholics and artificial contraception? Why are there so many rules? As I searched, a couple things happened. First, I found answers, good answers. Each time I researched a question and read what the Church actually taught, I was struck by how balanced and tempered the answers were. It was as if there were really smart people who had read, thought, and prayed about this stuff over the past two millennia and then wrote about it to pass it on to another generation. Crazy. I started to understand that, through my baptism, this rich faith was meant for me—it was my inheritance. The more that I studied, the more I discovered a world of resources beyond Google. I found podcasts by priests who were on fire for Jesus. I found books and articles by brilliant, holy theologians, many of them converts themselves. I found what I was looking for to feed my hunger, and I absorbed it like a sponge.

Yet I still didn't understand why all of this wasn't common knowledge. Why hadn't I learned it sooner? Why didn't my parents and their friends know this stuff? Actually, with the exception of my brilliant high school youth minister and a handful of my religion teachers, why didn't anyone know anything? It was clear that the men and women who were well versed in understanding the Catholic faith were few and far between, and those who did understand either had converted or had an extraordinary experience that propelled them to discover the faith on their own. What happened? How was such a treasure lost on entire generations of people?

Statistics are easy to cite. A Pew Research Center study revealed that for every one person entering the Catholic Church, 6.5 are leaving.[2] Of the seventy million people in the US who were raised Catholic, thirty-two million have fallen away from the Church.[3] These statistics are a snapshot of where we stand; they don't give us the context. The context lies in our shared history. Although today's Catholic climate has emerged from an infinite historical narrative, historians typically cite four shifts in American life that have shaped our modern Catholic situation.[4] These four shifts are in no way the entire story, but they do give us context. They are Catholicism at the nation's founding, after World War II, after the Second Vatican Council, and after the release of *Humanae Vitae*. I am not a historian, theologian, or sociologist, and I will not present these shifts as such, but I did find them helpful in understanding why the Church is the way it is today, and I hope you find them helpful too.

Early American Catholicism

At the beginning of our country's founding, Catholics generally came to America as lower-class immigrants. Here in their new home, Catholics were a persecuted minority group. The nation was made up of mostly Protestants who were suspicious of Catholics for their loyalty to the pope and misunderstood religious practices such as worshipping in Latin, venerating Mary, and practicing devotion to the saints. As with most immigrant groups during industrialization, Catholics gravitated toward one another, often forming ethnic communities with a deeply rooted Catholic identity where life revolved around the local parish. Priests and nuns served the Catholic population by establishing institutions. They built schools, churches, charities, and hospitals, through which much of Catholic life was funneled. The teachings and traditions of the Church were strong and passed on to subsequent generations through worship, education, culture, and socialization.[5]

World War II and the Postwar Era

During World War II, the walls between religious and ethnic communities started to break down. For the first time, the entire nation was united under the war effort. Men fought abroad with other men from every different place, background, and religion. Those at home were experiencing similar diversities as they worked together to support troops overseas. The war vastly changed the landscape of America, igniting a stronger sense of religious tolerance. American Catholics no longer identified with only the other Catholics they knew; rather, they identified with the American dream as the Catholic story of immigration began to morph into one of religious integration.

After World War II, the GI Bill was offered to returning soldiers. The bill's benefits included low-cost mortgages, low-interest loans to start a business or a farm, and payments toward tuition for former soldiers to attend college. The GI Bill allowed many Catholic men to climb economic and social ladders. In the postwar era, Catholics were no longer outsiders. They were normal Americans who were accepted, prominent, and numerous (by 1970 Catholics represented 24 percent of the population),[6] and they identified as such. The Catholic faith with its traditions was still important to many Catholics, but they also found themselves at the center of contemporary issues such as civil rights, the feminist movement, the sexual revolution, the changing dynamics of the family, and the disintegrating obligations of traditions.[7]

The Catholic rise to prominence culminated with the election of John. F. Kennedy, the first and only Catholic to be elected president. When asked about the involvement of his Catholic faith, Kennedy responded, "I am not the Catholic candidate for president. I am the Democratic Party's candidate for president, who happens also to be a Catholic. I do not speak for my church on public matters, and the church does not speak for me."[8]

This answer at first glance seems appropriate and innocuous since we Americans believe in the separation of church and state. Undoubtedly, though, Kennedy's statement was more than separation of church and state; it was separation of faith and reality. If one's religion has no bearing on everyday decision-making, it is powerless. Sadly, Kennedy's statement was a reflection of the growing sentiment of most Catholics: faith was private, and God was for Sundays.

As the 1960s came to a close, change had descended upon American life like a hurricane. The scene in which the baby boomers came of age was almost unrecognizable to their parents, who became adults twenty years prior in a vastly different culture. Now the fight for civil rights was at its height, and the sexual revolution was in motion as youth sought to break free from the chains of tradition and embrace the message of peace, experimentation, and free love.[9]

The Second Vatican Council

While cultural revolutions transformed the West, the Second Vatican Council occurred in Rome from 1962 to 1965. Catholic Church leaders from around the world came together to discuss how to present the truths of the faith to a contemporary world. The bishops present at Vatican II sought to answer the question of how to bring the Gospel to modern humans. The Council affirmed many of the Church's traditional teachings but also opened the doors to many changes, such as a focus on lay involvement, worship in the common tongue, changes to the liturgy for inclusion, and ecumenical dialogue.

Some theologians praise Vatican II while others criticize it. Either way, there's a vast agreement that Vatican II significantly changed the landscape of American Catholicism in an incredibly short amount of time. This unintentionally led to a cultural confusion about what it meant to be Catholic that is still being sorted out. As dioceses around the nation scrambled to implement these changes, they did little to educate their congregation about these changes and what they meant.

Immediately following Vatican II, the Church saw a steep decline in the number of priests and nuns. According to Christian Smith in *Young Catholic America*, "Between 1966 and 1969 alone, 3,413 American priests left the priesthood and 4,322 women religious left religious life. Between 1965 and 1971, the American Catholic Church lost 10 percent of its priests."[10] As the men and women who were most qualified to pass on the faith left their vocation, religious education and piety suffered tremendously. Young people saw religious authorities reject their vows in droves to go their own way.

In the midst of this mass exodus, it was lay men and women who picked up the slack of teaching catechesis—only they weren't nearly as educated or trained as those in religious life. Catholic education began to break down, as did reverence for the Church's traditions.[11]

Beginning in the late 1960s, the youth coming through Catholic schools, catechism classes, and Church faith formation had mostly received little more than the fumes of a robust faith. Today, we have had almost fifty years and four generations of young Catholics who have learned barely enough about their faith to fulfill their obligation to attend Sunday Mass and receive the sacraments. The brilliance of our faith that reveals the scriptures and tackles life's deepest questions has been buried under this series of cultural phenomena that has replaced a tradition of excellence with a tradition of ignorance. Peter Kreeft, a Catholic theologian, wrote that in the sixties the Church was struck with a swift disaster in which we lost a third of our priests, two-thirds of our nuns, and nine-tenths of our children's theological knowledge.[12] Even those who have a sincere love for God and a sincere love for the Church rarely know enough of the *whys* behind the *whats* of Catholicism to pass them on effectively.

Humanae Vitae

In 1968, in the wake of Vatican II, the Catholic Church was exploring its stance on artificial contraception as an acceptable means of family planning. Many Catholics waited anxiously for the Church to officially change its teaching and allow Catholics to use artificial birth control. Instead, the opposite happened: Pope Paul VI released *Humanae Vitae*, the encyclical that affirmed the Church's stance that artificial contraception is an immoral means of family planning. It was as if a bomb had dropped on the American Catholic Church, which only compounded the confusion felt by lay Catholics.

Many bishops, priests, and people in the pews decided not to follow the teachings of *Humanae Vitae*. In fact, many priests and bishops did not even read the document before signing an official letter of dissent.[13] The faithful could try to understand the stance of the Church and be faithful to its teachings, or they could follow their own way in the direction of modern culture. Most chose modern culture, as the controversy of *Humanae Vitae* gave rise to the "Cafeteria Catholic," and a general sentiment formed within churchgoers that Catholic teachings were optional. One did not have to believe the whole to be part of the culture. If the Second Vatican Council resulted in confusion about Catholicism, then it was *Humanae Vitae* that gave many Catholics an excuse to ignore the harder tenets of the faith.[14]

The Postmodern Result

Even as I am offering this very brief history, there are many more factors swirling around in my head that I cannot include. This is not a comprehensive study on the history of our American Church but a general snapshot of our story, which is in many ways remarkable. American Catholics are an immigrant success story and have done tremendous good in this nation. We have much to be proud of.

What I do hope to illuminate here, though, is how we have millions of Catholics who have left the Church with no desire to darken its doors ever again. The Catholic faith was once compelling enough to send thousands of people to a willing death for Jesus Christ; today it doesn't even compel many people to miss a football game to attend Mass. Where is the fire, the beauty, the fervor, the adventure seeking, and the risk-taking desire to know God and make him known to everyone?

In the book of Judges, Joshua, who led the nation of Israel into the Promised Land, died. Joshua's generation established the nation of Israel in the land of Canaan. They had seen the incredible works of the Lord, believed in him, and sought to be faithful to him. As they all died, however, a different generation arose. Judges 2:10–12 tells us,

> And all that generation also were gathered to their fathers; and there arose another generation after them, who did not know the LORD or the work which he had done for Israel. And the people of Israel did what was evil in the sight of the LORD and served the Baals; and they forsook the LORD, the God of their fathers, who had brought them out the land of Egypt; they went after other gods, from among the gods of the peoples who were round about them.

Today, we can say the same for our most recent generations. For years, Catholicism was passed on through a deep culture of tradition. As that tradition began to fade, the older generation did not intentionally pass on the faith of the next generation. As is predictable of the human heart, we forsook the Gospel message for the glamour of the American dream and our idols of comfort and prosperity. Jesus told us to take up our crosses, but many have found that too difficult in the land of opportunity, and so we settled for fulfilling obligations such as going to Mass on Sunday. Jesus quotes the prophet Isaiah and says in Matthew 15:8–9, "This people honors me with their lips, but their heart is far from me; in vain do they worship me, teaching as doctrines the precepts of men." Because of this, for years we have lost the heart of our true teachings. For at least four generations now, we have not known why we should believe, why Catholicism is sensible, or why we should follow all the Church's teachings. We have lost the story of our faith and so have lost the reasons.

Why I Stayed

In the summer of 2016, my husband had the opportunity to speak at an international Catholic conference in Austria. Always the adventurer, Jared decided that my seven-month-old, my brother-in-law, and I should meet him in Rome after the conference for vacation. There were a ton of reasons not to go: we didn't have that much money, we had a baby, and our lives had been crazy busy with travel, settling into marriage, and having our first child. What I really wanted was rest. In the end, though, Jared convinced me to consent on sheer persuasion and the fact that his ticket would be paid for. I packed up and got on a plane, baby in tow, to meet Jared in Rome.

The trip was like a second conversion experience for me. Every time we saw a new religious site, I could feel my smallness, as though I were standing in front of the Grand Canyon. How many men and women shed their blood so that I could know Jesus Christ thousands of years later? Countless heroes helped to spread the goodness of Christianity all over the world, and I was standing on the same ground on which they stood at one point in time, worshipping the same God that I did, in the same Mass that I do, in the same faith that I have. Each moment for me, accompanied by good pasta and good wine, was a sober realization that the story of Catholicism is the compilation of an infinite number of unique persons, individually choosing God and letting him write their lives. I realized again how lucky I am to be part of it.

While we were in Rome, we went on the Vatican's Scavi tour, which takes you through the ruins underneath St. Peter's Basilica, the primary site of papal liturgies and celebrations. The tour will eventually lead you to the tomb of St. Peter, which lies directly under the tabernacle of the church above it. The tour was wonderful. My brother-in-law Adam and I walked through while my husband stayed with our daughter. Our tour guide was a dry-humored, sarcastic British man who had us laughing the entire way through. His demeanor changed, however, as we approached St. Peter's tomb. He became more reverent in his attitude, more passionate in his speech. He explained to us that each Roman mausoleum we had seen before contained a couple of Roman coins, which would have been left by family members of the deceased to help them cross the River Styx. As the excavators approached St. Peter's tomb, they found up to twelve hundred coins from all over the world. This had been a pilgrimage site before it was filled in for more building.

Adam kept repeating the same question after we completed the tour: "How does nobody know about any of this stuff?" But the experience really took hold in my heart a few days later as I was praying through the daily readings. On this particular day, the gospel reading was from Matthew 16, when Jesus gives Peter the keys to the kingdom. It's the passage in the Bible from which Catholics claim St. Peter is the first pope. Having just seen St. Peter's bones under his basilica, I read the story with new eyes.

Jesus asks the apostles, "Who do you say that I am?" Peter responds, "You are the Christ, the Son of the living God." Jesus says to Peter, "Blessed are you, Simon Bar-Jona! For flesh and blood has not revealed this to you, but my Father who is in heaven. And I tell you, you are Peter, and on this rock I will build my church, and the powers of death shall not prevail against it" (15–18).

Did you catch that? "You are Peter, and on this rock I will build my church." Yes, Jesus made Peter the pope and the foundation of the Catholic Church, but he also actually built his church on Peter. *Mind. Blown.*

This is why I stayed in the Church. Our God is so complete. He is so literal, and his hand can be seen in all of history in every part of the world. The teachings of the Church might seem a bit crazy at times, but doesn't every adventure story? When I decided to continue to be a Catholic, I knew I had to find answers. I could not profess something in which I didn't fully believe, and so I set out on a journey to make sense of it all. Yes, it is a mystery and belief does come from faith, but if humanity is a reflection of the nature of

God and he revealed himself to us through his Son who became a human, there must be good and reasonable answers. And there are.

So here are just a few things I learned in my studies that made sense of the many questions I have had continuously. They might not answer everything for you, but they were helpful to me.

What Is the Trinity?

The Trinity is "the central mystery of Christian faith and life" (CCC, 234). As Christians we believe in one God, who is also three persons. Try wrapping your mind around that one with complete understanding—it's not possible. The Trinity cannot be understood only by reason. It is a mystery that we cannot, in our limited minds, understand completely. Yet reason is our pathway to beholding such a mystery with appropriate awe and wonder, as opposed to dismissing the statement and moving on with our lives.

If God has left traces of his Trinitarian being in his work of creation and revealed himself in revelation, then we can look to each of these things to understand this mystery beyond the statement "It is a mystery." I would even argue it is crucial that we try, for it is in grasping what we can about these things that we can start to understand the nature of God and how we are called to live with him.

"Beloved, let us love one another; for love is of God, and he who loves is born of God and knows God" (1 Jn 4:7). *God is love.* This is the simplest, most accurate description of God that exists. All of salvation history occurred to write this truth on our hearts. Love by its nature shares itself; it creates. This is one of the ways that God has left a trace of his Trinitarian life on creation because we see this nature unfold within humanity.

Think about what happens when two people fall in love. First, they date. They share their own lives with each other, and they tell anyone who will listen about their new relationship. Immediately, something new is created that must be shared. If that love continues to grow and the couple decides to get married, they choose to enter into another new creation that it is meant to be permanent. The two become one and a family is created. The love of the new husband and wife, made concrete in the sexual embrace, is meant to lead to an entirely new person, a complete new human with an eternal soul, unique, totally separate from his or her parents and infinitely loved by God.

God is father and creator, and he is the origin of everything. Jesus is the Word of God made flesh, and he reveals the nature of the Father. The Holy Spirit is the revelation of the perfect relationship that exists between Father and Son. He is the spirit of Truth that proceeds from the Father and the Son. Three persons who reveal one nature. If God is love, the Trinity is the perfect exchange of that love. God the Father pours his love out perfectly and completely on God the Son, who returns it perfectly and completely. Out of that exchange of love proceeds the personification of that love, which is the Holy Spirit.

The three persons of the Trinity are consubstantial, which means they are of the same essence. They exist outside of time but were revealed to humanity within time: God the Father in the beginning, the Son of God in the Incarnation, and the Holy Spirit at Pentecost. Is your head about to explode? Mine is as I am writing this. Our attempt to grasp the Trinity in history should lead us to kneel before the mystery. On one level it makes sense. On another level, I have to sit back and marvel at a God who has made himself accessible and is still so *other*.

In the scriptures, Jesus tells us that the two greatest commandments are love the Lord your God with all your heart, all your mind, and all your soul and love your neighbor as yourself. With so many definitions of love floating around, what does that even mean? Who is God that we should love him? What sort of love, exactly, is he asking of us? He is asking us to become lovers in the way that he is a lover. He desires that we live a life striving to love as he loves, in total self-gift and open to creation. The more that we understand God's nature and character, the more concretely we know what we are striving for when we are called to "love our neighbor as ourselves." God has given us a faith that helps us navigate our everyday lives. He has revealed the mystery so that we can know him as well as we can on this side of heaven. These mysteries, properly held, reveal the meaning of our lives and feed our desire to know our creator even more.

What Is the Incarnation?

Christmas of 2010 may be the first time I ever actually listened to the words of "O Holy Night," you know, that Christmas song that has been recorded by everyone from Nat King Cole to Mariah Carey to NSYNC. So during, let's say, the 110th time I heard this song when I was twenty-three, my jaw hit the floor. The first two lines of the song reveal the truth of the Incarnation, simply and poetically: "Long lay the world in sin and error pining. Till he appeared and the soul felt its worth." This one phrase sums up just how much the Incarnation meant on a cosmic level. Our souls had forgotten their worth, until he, Jesus Christ, the Son of the living God, was born into this world. How would our celebration of Christmas fundamentally shift if we believed this? How would our sense of self be different? Take heart, friend. Just as God has revealed his nature in the life of the Trinity, he has revealed the meaning of the Incarnation. Remember that God is not separate from reason; he created a rational world, and so his mysteries are also revealed to us.

Remember the bad news of the Gospel? I am talking about the part where God created humans out of his own sheer goodness to participate in his own blessed life and we totally screwed up by rejecting him to go our own way. That is where all of our problems started. Because of our sin, there is nothing we can do to get back into a life in God's good graces. We created the problem, but we cannot fix the problem. It's as if we once lived at the top of a mountain that was infinitely high and fell off. Now, we can try to climb for eternity, but we can never reach the top. No good work, no prayer, and no amount of atonement can do it.

God, therefore, in his goodness, answered the problem with the Incarnation. Only he could fix the problem by extending himself down to us. Infinity became finite, and Jesus Christ, the Word Made Flesh, and the indwelling of the nature of divinity and the nature of humanity, lived the experience of humanity to completion without ever sinning. If we sit with this fact, it's remarkable. Can you imagine going through your entire life *never* having committed the smallest grievance against perfection? It's impossible. Jesus did it. In 2 Corinthians 8:9, we read, "For you know the grace of our Lord Jesus Christ, that though he was rich, yet for your sake he became poor, so that by his poverty you might become rich." In the birth, death, and resurrection of Jesus Christ, God extended his hand down the infinite mountain and pulled us back to where we belong. Ephesians 2:4–5 says, "But God, who is rich in mercy, out of the great love with which he loved us, even when we were dead through our trespasses, made us alive together with Christ (by grace you have been saved)." In other words, "He appeared and the soul felt its worth."

It doesn't make sense that we can make ourselves right with God in any way except through his mercy, so our gratitude should be endless. The Father's love goes as deep as the mystery of the Incarnation. Our understanding of this mystery should inform every part of our lives, from our sense of worth to our comprehension of how God feels about us and our grasp of the nature of the relationship between God and humanity to our everyday decision-making.

What Is the Purpose of the Church?

As religion and reality have become increasingly separated in American culture, we have lost our understanding of religion's purpose altogether. We're confused when Church leaders comment on current events, politics, and seemingly secular cultural questions. But at its heart, religion is meant to be a foundation for life, not an extra. It's not a feel-good practice that we can take or leave according to our tastes; it is meant to inform everything, and so it can speak to every part of life.

According to the teachings of the Catholic Church, God is the origin of all creation. God in his goodness created the world to work in a certain order that would reflect his own divine life and allow humanity to live and walk as closely with him as possible. Because we are created in his image, we thrive best when we live according to the order of life that he established.

In this original order, there were four proper relationships that existed (*CCC* 376). These were right relationships between humanity and God, human and self, human and other humans, and human and nature; in all these relationships, it was easy for humans to give the gift of themselves. After the Fall, that order was broken. Humanity is no longer inclined to be selfless; we are inclined to be selfish, and those original relationships no longer naturally flourish: humanity is not inclined to worship God as was intended. Each human's relationship with him- or herself is now complicated; humans use other humans for personal gain, and humans and nature war with each other instead of existing in harmony. All of these consequences are easy to see in our everyday lives. Just think about that one thing you want to do but keep failing at; your will wants one thing, but your passions lead you toward another. Or just look at the news: there is evidence of these broken relationships everywhere, as we kill, lie, steal, and harm the earth.

God, in his goodness, sent Jesus Christ to restore what had been lost. In the life, death, and resurrection of Jesus, we are redeemed from this brokenness. We have been restored to life with the Father and can, through his grace, live a life of restored order. This, of course, doesn't mean it isn't a battle. We often find ourselves in an internal war between sin and virtue, between desiring God and desiring empty pleasure, and between wanting to be a self-gift and wanting to live for our own gain. But Jesus can defeat the darkness within us, and it becomes easier to live as God intended, walking closely with him and thriving as we were meant to.

This, my friend, is the purpose of the Church. The Church exists to spread the Gospel message as Truth, not optional fiction. Every single practice and belief within the life of the Church is meant to bring the Gospel message to those who have not heard it and direct those who have heard it on how to apply the Gospel to every aspect of their lives. The Church weighs in on current events, politics, and cultural issues because the Gospel is meant to transform our response to them. The Church cares about how you live your life because "there is a way which seems right to a man, but its end is the way to death" (Prv 14:12), and there is a way to live that leads us to life. We can miss Truth, and people do it all the time.

The Church exists to make saints, and saints live the most incredible, joyful lives of all. This is the purpose of Catholicism, to bring us into the reality of God and to guide us into the fullness of joy. Catholicism was never meant to be ancillary to real life; it is meant to be the foundation of our lives from which everything else flows. It is our road map to life and our path back to heaven. We can and should wrestle with the Church teachings, but only with the proper understanding of what they are trying to do in the first place.

When we know the *whys* behind the *whats*, we can make informed decisions. I have rarely spoken to someone who has left the Church because they flat-out rejected its teachings with a full understanding of what those teachings are. More often than not, people leave because the *what* of our faith rubbed them the wrong way but they never learned the *why*. The *why* is everything. Knowing the reasons behind belief allow believers to take the leap of faith that accompanies the mystery of religion. I stayed in the Church because my soul came to life more and more every time I learned a *why*. The more that I received spiritual nourishment, the more clearly I could see the difference between a life with God and a life without him. The more I came into contact with Truth, the more I fell in love with it and the more easily I could discern it from a lie. My hope for you, friend, is that you recognize that longing in your heart and a deep, nagging desire for God and his Truth.

4.
Letting Go **
of Unpracticed
Preaching

What I Experienced

Remember when I took a side job working photo booths at parties? That job brought me to many different experiences because, well, there are many different types of parties. One of these parties took me down to Ybor City in Tampa. I hadn't been there in months, and I was excited to be a part of the sights and sounds again for a night—my evening social life was starting to resemble that of a seventy-year-old prayer quilt ministry leader.

On the drive, I wondered what to expect from the party; it was for a former NFL player's sixteen-year-old son, and a whole nightclub was reserved. I was also told that MTV would be there filming, so I expected nothing less than the best food and drink accompanied by the spectacle of teenagers with way too much money at their disposal, exploring the world of pubescent over-sexualization. *How interesting*, I thought. *How fun!*

It was everything I expected it to be—except that it wasn't fun. I hadn't anticipated just how depressing it would be to watch the free-flowing depravity run amok over kids who were barely old enough to drive. The nightclub had a full-service, top-shelf bar that was elevated from the dance floor. It was roped off as a space for the parents to hang out in their red carpet attire while they drank their fancy drinks and watched their children mimic them on the floor below. The dance floor was complete with all the lights, sounds, and cameras you would expect. The teenagers wore clothing that matched their parents', only more revealing because the kids were younger and "sexier." They also drank out of their flasks instead of glassware and in the bathrooms instead of at the bar, and made out in the photo booth. The music was so loud I couldn't have a conversation with my coworker, so I just watched. I watched the lack of smiles in the room. I watched the look of discomfort on so many of the girls' faces as the young boys took unwelcome interest in them. I listened to the lyrics of the songs that played and cringed at all the times I had bought into this exact same lifestyle, looking for life, joy, and fulfillment in a dark room. I wanted so much more for these kids and their parents. I wanted to live in a culture that invites us into true joy instead of numbing pleasure.

I left that night with a depression that took me days to shake. Even as I sit here now, years later, the scene replays in my mind and I feel a remnant of emptiness. One small detail that stood out to me starkly that night remains in my memory. It was the "rope" between the parents and the kids. The adults who threw the party knew exactly what to expect. They reserved a club in the party district of Tampa, spent thousands of dollars, and invited MTV to this party. The law against underage drinking and rules about barriers around bars could be gotten around with a wink and a nod and a rope. They established a culture that let their kids know that parents don't care whether they follow that law.

To top all of this off, the majority of these kids at the party went to the two local Catholic schools. I wasn't surprised. In fact, I somewhat expected it; it was just another point of duplicity. The adults in the room gave lip service to their Catholic faith by enroll-ing their kids in Catholic schools but lived a life that didn't align with Christian principles. Just as the rope between the bar and the dance floor was merely a fake salute to a law the teenagers knew the parents really didn't believe, the teens could also see this duplicity in their parents when they made vague overtures about following a religion they so clearly didn't choose to follow themselves.

Hypocrisy is easy to spot regardless of your age, but the effect of hypocrisy is especially powerful on the young, who see clearly the difference between talk and action in the adults who are leading them. Think about your own upbringing. Did you ever see cognitive dissonance, where an adult who was a religious role model in your life made choices that looked far different from what they were preaching to you? I remember discussing cohabitation with a role model who had repeatedly told me that cohabitation is wrong, a sin according to the Church. We were talking about a certain couple who had been dating for many years, and I asked, "Oh, are they living together?" The response was, "Well, they are in their thirties." Without missing a beat, I thought, *Morality has an expiration date?* I learned in that conversation that my role model didn't actually believe cohabitation was sinful or that the Church held the truth on this issue; she believed that limiting cohabitation kept young people safe, but once you hit a certain age it was fine.

You may have absolutely no problem with cohabitation. Most people don't. My point is not to get into a discussion about the pros and cons of living together before marriage. My point is that one of my religious role models was telling me the teachings of the Church and directing me to follow them, but that conversation revealed even she wasn't convinced of the validity of these religious rules. If she wasn't, then why should I be?

For years many of us, no matter our age, have watched our religious role models fail to practice what they preach in major ways. I'm not talking about the human brokenness that we all experience as we try to be holy. Everyone fails and falls, and everyone deserves mercy. I am talking about deliberate, unapologetic unbelief that reveals itself in the choices of the same people who are pushing vaguely traditional religious rules on their children.

According to Christian Smith in *Young Catholic America*, "In order for Catholic teenagers to maintain or achieve a high level of religious commitment and practice as they become emerging adults, three primary factors are key. First, teens must have strong bonds to religiously committed and supportive family and friends. Parents are the most important."[1] Parents' lifestyles, whether they talk about faith and whether they live it, it is a deciding factor in how their children will feel about religion. It's so important that the *Catechism of the Catholic Church* says, "The role of parents in education is of such importance that it is almost impossible to provide an adequate substitute. The right and the duty of parents to educate their children are primordial and inalienable" (2221).

For years now, parents have abdicated this duty to school and culture while chasing their own fleeting pleasures. Maybe you have experienced something such as this growing up. Your family went to church once a week, but God was rarely mentioned outside of the Sunday service. Or you knew adults who were quick to talk about God, Jesus, the Bible, or the rules of the Catholic Church and were mean, judgmental, or the first to engage in gossip. You knew a man who was on the finance committee for the Church and lectured on Sundays, and then learned he was cheating on his wife. You knew parents who baptized their kids but did nothing to own the faith for themselves. You knew teachers at a Catholic school who partied hard on the weekends.

There is mercy to be given here. Everyone is fallen, and not even the worst sin can keep the repentant from God. Yet when the young see a spiritual leader who is an unrepentant sinner, they get a powerful message: God can't make people happy because, if he could, the people in charge would be following the rules. And Christianity is a practical myth meant to serve us when convenient or make us feel good.

Matthew Warner, in his article "Why the World Doesn't Take Catholicism Seriously," wrote: "My parents' generation left the Church without leaving the pews. And now they wonder why their kids find it silly to stand in the pews of a church they never really understood professing creeds they never really believed."[2] In my years in ministry, I have spoken with countless parents who are devastated that their kids left the Catholic Church. It is heartbreaking to see their anguish, but tragically, in my conversations with them, they usually reveal they gave their children very little that would make them think Catholicism offered an attractive way of life. They took their kids to church and sent them to Catholic school and expected that to be enough. It wasn't. We needed to see the example lived out, and in general, we didn't. So we left.

What I Learned

One of my favorite Protestant pastors is Matt Chandler out of the Village Church in Dallas, Texas. I discovered him when I heard a clip of his preaching on my mission trip to Prague, and I listened to him weekly for the next seven years. His yelling may not be for you, but if you like unabashed truth delivered with the desperate conviction of someone who doesn't care if it makes you uncomfortable, he is your guy. I do not know him personally, but I can tell from the way he speaks that he is seeking a life of godly integrity and total transformation by the Holy Spirit. Chandler isn't perfect, but he has set his life up in a way that clearly reveals his priorities to observers. He honors his wife while being honest about their struggles. Every single sermon that he preaches focuses on the Gospel message, and it is clear from the way he runs his church that he makes decisions based on what will glorify God, not himself. In his own conversion, Chandler came face-to-face with his personal depravity against the greatness, glory, and mercy of our Lord Jesus Christ, and it changed everything for him. This is a man who understands the true nature of worship, and it was through his preaching that I came to understand it as well.

Children can be raised in Christian homes for years and never experience the Good News of the Gospel, which means they never understand the meaning and consequence of worship. Growing up, I knew we were supposed to love and worship God, but I never saw what that looked like. What is worship? Who worships? How does it affect us? Listening to Pastor Chandler yell his way through these explanations on worship gave me a new understanding: In order for us to truly make progress in life, we have to know what drives our behavior. Our behavior is a direct manifestation of what we worship in the depths of our hearts, and it's out of worship that we develop bad habits and addictions or joys and freedoms.

So, what is worship? Humanity worships by nature. We don't choose to do it; rather, it is an involuntary action of the human soul to serve something outside of itself. We recognize an emptiness within ourselves, and we are driven to fill it with temporary pleasures. St. Paul expresses this feeling in Romans 7:15–19:

> I do not understand my own actions. For I do not do what I want, but I do the very thing I hate. Now if I do what I do not want, I agree that the law is good. So then it is no longer I that do it, but sin which dwells within me. For I know that nothing good dwells within me, that is, in my flesh. I can will what is right, but I cannot do it. For I do not do the good I want, but the evil I do not want is what I do.

And so, out of our desire to become who we were made to be and to fill the ache inside of us, we look to what is on the outside to fill it. Once we find that thing we think will make up for what we lack within, we give ourselves over to it in service with the hope that it will serve us back. This is worship. We give that thing power and we place it above ourselves, hoping it will fill our emptiness.

We can worship anything we think has the power to make us into the image of ourselves as we were made to be. Our contemporary objects of idolatry tend to be money, success, relationships, comfort, and body image. We look to these things to make up for what we are missing, hoping they will give us happiness, peace, fulfillment, and joy. They never do. Psalm 115 says it perfectly: "Why should the nations say, 'Where is their God?' Our God is in the heavens; he does whatever he pleases. Their idols are silver and gold, the work of men's hands. They have mouths, but do not speak; eyes, but do not see. They have ears, but do not hear; noses, but do not smell. They have hands, but do not feel; feet, but do not walk; and they do not make a sound in their throat. *Those who make them are like them; so are all who trust in them*" (2–8, emphasis added).

Did you catch that last sentence? That is a serious mic drop. Those idols are dead, they are objects, and all who worship them will be like them! We can never be bigger than or better than the gods we worship. If we worship money, we will only ever be worth what is in our bank account—and it will never be enough because there could always be more. We will soon find ourselves sacrificing important things in service of our idols, and slowly this worship, of which we may be barely aware, will be driving our behavior. In our search for a worthy god, we have placed ourselves in bondage to little tyrants. It ends up being the same story over and over again with a different false god leading us to false comfort. If we worship romantic relationships, our worth will completely rely on whether we have a significant other and how that person treats us. We will find ourselves looking less and less like who we want to become and more and more like the idol we serve.

After learning about worship, I could see the consequences of idolatry all over my own life. For years, I really liked the idea of God and religion, but I didn't see God as the source of my fulfillment. I never truly worshipped him. I worshipped image and success. I thought if I could just have the perfect image—physically and materially—I would be worthy of love, and if I could just be successful to the world, everyone would be proud of me. This led to lots of disorder in my life. In college, I became preoccupied with achieving a life of wealth and fun. You know, the kind you see on the TV, the kind that I saw the parents and kids chasing after at my photo booth gig in Ybor City. I was also a slave to my body's appearance, from fashion to fitness, and I developed a terrible relationship with food: I didn't actually enjoy what I ate because I was too busy feeling guilty from overeating. I would rollercoaster diet and work out like crazy to try to undo what my bad eating habits had done. I rated my "date-ability" on how thin I felt that day. I constantly compared myself to other women and was jealous of those who were thinner or prettier than me, which of course left me dealing with profound insecurity. The idols I worshipped gave me neurosis, jealousy, and suspicion, and they lowered my moral standards; they never set me free. Freedom only comes from true worship. Freedom only comes from God.

Looking back, I actually had everything I was pining for, but none of it brought me joy because I was so busy serving dead, unattainable idols. I was in shape, I had cute clothes, and I had great friends; I also broke almost every promise I made to myself about morality in service to these tyrants. As I gave myself over to my little gods, I became less and less myself and more a caricature of some forgettable extra in a poorly written party movie. My idols did not serve me; they turned me into a mockery of myself.

Think about your behavior and the behavior of those around you. Can you see the effects? Think back to the good or bad examples set for you by the adults in your life. Think about their behavior. What do they worship? What do you worship? The hypocritical role models in my life had the same problem I had. The idols of our age are attractive, and while most of these adults had a sense of fidelity to religion or even a desire to love God, they worshipped something else on a daily basis and the disordered effects eventually shone through. False worship is the foundation of a duplicitous, hypocritical life—and it is honestly hard to avoid. We all have our little idols. It only the grace of God, the way of holiness, the desire, the will, and the actions we take to worship the living God, that can break us of our idolatry, transform us from the inside, and make us into the saints that others will want to follow. For most of us, however, we pay lip service to God and worship something else with our lives, clueless of its effects on us and the people who look up to us the most.

Why I Stayed

I often think about the world that surrounded those who came before us. Until recently, that world would have been much quieter. Imagine being alone in your thoughts for much of the day. Imagine being more familiar with the voice of God than the sound of music. Could you imagine seeing the stars every single night, with no light pollution to hide them away? King David would have seen this over and over during his years as a young shepherd. In an experience of unadulterated beauty, David understood, as he stood beneath the stars, exactly who he was compared to the Almighty God. In Psalm 8:3–5, he wrote, "When I look at thy heavens, the work of thy fingers, the moon and the stars which thou have established; what is man that thou art mindful of him, and the son of man that thou dost care for him? Yet thou hast made him little less than God, and dost crown him with glory and honor."

Seriously, who are we that God would keep us in mind when most of the time we don't keep him in mind? When we fell from grace, we fell far. Still, regardless of our sin, God keeps us in mind. He gave us a place in the universe, lower than the angels and above everything else.

When we direct our worship toward the living God, we begin to see reality clearly because there is nothing blocking our view. He orders our disordered hearts, elevates us to where we belong, and frees us to experience true joy. True worship leads to true joy; no other path will lead us there.

His Church exists to lead us into a life of true worship, not just with our heads or our hearts, but in every aspect of our lives. The Church shows us how to live life abundantly, by sharing with us the Good News of the Gospel of Jesus Christ and showing us how to live that Gospel. If Jesus Christ is the center of history and our redeemer, then he has something to say about how we treat other people, how we spend our time, how we run our families, how we conduct business, how we handle our money, and the list goes on.

Of course, that doesn't mean that following the teachings of the Church is easy. We tend to have a million problems with the morality of the Church because we like our little gods. It is always easier to serve an idol at first. It is only later that it can feel impossible to break its hold on us. It is always more difficult to choose to live a life in worship of God at first. The joy, peace, and confidence tend to come only after the sacrifice has been made.

I stayed in the Catholic Church because I knew that, left to my own devices, I would wander from God. The Church, in its "antiquated" teachings, leads me down the path of true worship and into wisdom. My joy, my fulfillment, my ability to love, and the state of my soul in eternity depend on my worship. It matters too much to get it wrong. The teachings of Catholicism have challenged me to desire more. Over the past ten years, I have worked diligently to rid myself of my little gods. In worshipping the one true God,

I have found immense freedom. God in his goodness and mercy has been reorienting my heart toward him. The journey isn't always fun, but it is definitely the adventure that my soul desires. In God, I have found the love for which I long, and his goodness is revealed to me in all of his creation.

Most of us have been given a "Jesus vaccine" in one way or another: We got just enough Jesus to know that we don't want more. We have seen the generation that came before us acknowledge God only with their lips but deny him by their actions, and we have rightly rejected this example. I would submit to you, however, that the solution is not to deny God with either our actions or our lips! Look to those who have been faithful to the Church, and judge for yourself according to the fruit of their lives. You will not be disappointed.

My number one hope for you, as your dear friend, is that you fall in love with God. I will tell you that over and over again because I have seen that a life lived in love with God is the best life there is. I also hope that one day you see that the teachings of the Catholic Church, when followed, turn men and women, broken by original sin, into saints. This framework of prayer, penance, joy, and suffering all for the sake of God's glory turns everyday humans into powerful heroes. It brings dignity to the shamed, joy to the sorrowful, encouragement to the brokenhearted, and true, yes true, fulfillment. It doesn't give life meaning, but it reveals life's meaning to all who take notice.

Our world does not need more individuals who are reflecting the cheap glamour and drama of their modern idols. We do not need one more generation raised in the confusion of mass hypocrisy. We need saints. We need men and women who wake up every day passionately striving to live and worship rightly. We need marriages that are holy and families that truly love one another. This is the kind of life and witness that would bring life and joy, true joy, back into our society.

5.

Facing a Hypocritical Hierarchy

What I Experienced

As I packed for that wonderful Rome trip, the one that changed my life even though I didn't want to go, I decided to watch something educational about the Vatican. I vaguely remembered seeing promotions for a documentary titled *Inside the Vatican*, which I thought was a tour of the Vatican that tells you what's upstairs in the papal palace, where there are secret passages, which pope is buried where, that kind of stuff. With a quick internet search, a PBS special, *Secrets of the Vatican*, came up, and I eagerly pressed play. This documentary revealed many secrets of the Vatican to be sure, but the subject matter did not illuminate the nooks, crannies, and histories of the place itself. Instead, it was an exposé on the double lives that many priests lead and a look inside the scandals of the Vatican Bank. As you can imagine, it was devastating. I didn't want to believe the stories, and yet I knew much of what the documentary said was true. Too many of our leaders have been devastatingly careless while using their vocation for selfish gain, ruthlessly destroying the lives of the faithful. I watched as much as I could handle and then slowly, sadly, shut my computer, knowing that I would walk into St. Peter's Square suspicious of the supposed "guardians of our faith" who reside in Rome.

I was only fourteen when the first major sex abuse scandal of the Catholic Church broke in 2002, and I don't remember it that well. I digested the scandal with the outrage of a distant spectator, the same way that fair-weather fans would handle their team's losses. It mattered, but not as much as it should have. I recall hearing specific details and being appalled at the incompetence of the hierarchy. I remember losing trust in members of the clergy as well. I didn't necessarily think they were all sexual predators, but I do remember thinking that, at some level, they were all fake. My journey away from and back to the Catholic Church, however, had almost nothing to do with the scandals. So watching *Secrets of the Vatican* was one of the first times I revisited, up close, the rot that has festered within the culture of our Church's leaders, and I could barely face it.

The scene that I remember the most from this horrifying documentary was the footage submitted by Carmelo Abbate, an undercover reporter who started investigating the double lives of the priests in the Vatican. Knowing he would need undeniable proof to accuse men with the power of the Vatican behind them, Abbate wore a hidden camera on a night that he was invited out with clergy members. They went out to clubs where the priests were well known and ended the night sleeping at the home of Abbate's friend. His friend disappeared into a bedroom with one of the priests while Abbate slept in another room. The next morning the priest emerged from the bedroom and celebrated Mass in the home. As the documentary showed the secret footage of this priest celebrating Mass, I felt sick. Sin can deceive us so deeply that we are split down the middle, and somehow, some way, we are able to justify our behavior when our hypocrisy is blatantly seen by all those around us.[1]

As I turned off the documentary, I tried to wince away what faced me. How many lives have been ruined, the face of God marred by those trusted with revealing him to the world? I had always cared about the scandals and had shown righteous disgust when the topic came up, but I had to face them in a new way. I believe that Jesus Christ left for us a Church, a church that, despite its many faults, I had come to love. This Church is supposed to be the realization of Jesus' command to "go and make disciples" for every generation. Over time, it has become a den for the devil. How does one even begin to grapple with such a problem?

Two years later, my husband and I were visiting friends in Philadelphia when the news of the Pittsburgh report broke. Jared started to read the details of the report aloud, and that same sickness, only more pronounced, came over me again. "Stop," I told him. "Details like this shouldn't even exist." He did stop, but I eventually learned those details anyway.

For years I have said that sin makes people boring, and I believe that. Sin is not creative; it only twists what God in his goodness has created. The atrocities committed by our shepherd priests felt different though. While the sins themselves were not particularly creative, in the sense that they are the same sort of sexual immorality that has existed since the beginning of time, the details of these crimes dripped with wicked creativity. This evil seemed to have a personality; these priests were actively cooperating with the demonic in such a way that the devil could make a mockery of God and all that is holy. After all, he exists to kill, steal, and destroy.

Later that day, I was on a walk and listening to one of my favorite podcasters, who isn't a Catholic but would consider himself Catholic-friendly, talk about the problems in our house of God. I felt hopeless at his words. Hearing an outsider's perspective on the crisis, an outsider who I pray one day becomes Catholic, sent my heart into my feet. So many good people have been deeply hurt by this, and it seems as if the perpetrators didn't care very much. How do we even begin to fix such a deep-seated problem? I probably looked as if I was listening to rap as I threw my hands down, repeatedly unable to contain my righteous indignation. Again, no words. Again, total confusion. Again, anger and rage.

As the weeks went on, the story of Theodore McCarrick unfolded in the media as well: another snake allowed to lurk in the house
of God. His offenses were a well-known secret in the Church, and
he rose to the rank of cardinal. As the conversations continued
and the statistics emerged of just how much promiscuity, sexual
malfeasance, and impropriety happens in the Church leadership,
the reality started to make sense to me. I've been in the presence of
priests and religious and wondered why they ever entered religious
life in the first place—they didn't seem to love God.

And why would someone would give up a "normal" life if they
don't love God? Being a priest involves celibacy, obedience, and
often a life of poverty. Why give up sex and a family for any other
reason than that you love God, want to serve him and his people,
and see the priesthood as the best way for you to live your call?
During my time working in the Church, however, I realized men
have entered the priesthood for reasons that are not the noble sacrifice of spreading the Gospel. These include being taken care of by
the Church, getting a position of power upon ordination, gaining
the opportunity for advancement, becoming respected by your
community, avoiding the demands of marriage, and being able to
feed your sexual appetites regardless of your vows.

Jesus himself criticized men who sought spiritual authority
for selfish reasons. He saw into the hearts of the men of his time,
and he knew the future. In Matthew 23:2–7 and 13, he calls out
this sinfulness:

> The scribes and the Pharisees sit on Moses' seat; so prac-
> tice and observe whatever they tell you, but not what
> they do; for they preach, but do not practice. They bind
> heavy burdens, hard to bear, and lay them on men's
> shoulders; but they themselves will not move them with
> their finger. They do all their deeds to be seen by men;
> for they make their phylacteries broad and their fring-
> es long, and they love the place of honor at feasts and
> the best seats in the synagogues, and salutations in the
> market places, and being called rabbi by men. . . . But
> woe to you, scribes and Pharisees, hypocrites! because
> you shut the kingdom of heaven against men; for you

> neither enter yourselves, nor allow those who would
> enter to go in.

The hypocrisy of those with the collar is a significant reason behind the departure of the masses from Catholicism. There is no defense for it. And beyond those who have been wounded directly or indirectly by clergy abuse, many Catholics are rightly disgusted by the Church's attempt to shield abusive clergy. According to Bishop Robert Barron in his *Letter to a Suffering Church*, the Church spent four billion dollars to cover up this scandal. Four billion.[2] Pick your mouth up off the floor and imagine the good that could have been done with the generous donations made in good faith by the men and women in the pews. Think of the millions of people who have left the Church because of these scandals; they've had every reason to do so.

What I Learned

Would you know the proper way to greet the pope if you met him today? I would not, although I learned it once during an etiquette training. Yes, as a missionary, I learned how to hold a fork at a nice meal, to dance with the opposite sex, and naturally, to greet a Church official according to his rank. I think you are supposed to bend a specific knee and kiss a specific hand, but I'm actually not sure. What I am confident about though is how annoyed I became as we learned this small piece of etiquette.

The teacher clicked through a PowerPoint presentation and eventually landed on a slide with a picture of a bishop and Pope Benedict. As he walked us through the greeting of a Church official, I felt the negativity rising within me. I had only been back on the Catholic train for two years, and I didn't understand the point of the Church's hierarchical structure. Why is there so much pomp and circumstance in the power structures of our Church if these men are supposed to be servants?

Unable to shake my frustration, I went to Confession to talk it out with a priest whom I greatly respect. "Father, the other day

I was sitting in class, and we learned the proper way to greet the pope and members of the clergy," I started. "I don't understand why it matters. Why is there an officially proper way to greet the pope today when our very first pope was crucified upside down because he did not see himself as worthy to be crucified like Jesus? Why don't I see this humble attitude today?" With patience and love, the priest responded, "Mallory, as a priest, I am subject to the authority of men who make decisions that I sometimes do not respect. What I have to remember is that I have made a vow of obedience, and I exist as a priest within the Church that Jesus himself set up. It is flawed, but I can become holy and help others become holy within it. That is my job, and so I can deal with the rest."

I realized that I was focusing on the wrong things. My millennial senses are still a touch offended when I think of some of the practices of the institutional Catholic Church. Still, I recognize that none of the things that cause me to bristle even come close to nullifying the truth of the Church's teachings. There is a place for high honor in our society, and I can accept that men who have given their lives to the Church deserve our humble praise. They should accept it with humility, always pointing to the glory of God. But what about everything else? Why do we, as the Body of Christ, have to exist in an institution in the first place? Why can't it just be "Jesus and me"? Wouldn't that be holier?

Well, first, Jesus established the Church. And second, if we didn't have an institution, we would set one up anyway. As G. K. Chesterton comments in his novel *Manalive*,

> It is the fashion to talk of institutions as cold and cramping things. The truth is that when people are in exceptionally high spirits, really wild with freedom and invention, they always must, and they always do, create institutions. When men are weary they fall into anarchy; but while they are gay and vigorous they invariably make rules. This, which is true of all the churches and republics of history, is also true of the most trivial parlour game or the most unsophisticated meadow romp. We are never free until some institution frees us; and liberty cannot exist till it is declared by authority.[3]

Humans distrust institutions, often with good reason. If corruption sets in, these institutions become harmful. This is true of all churches, governments, and anything else that can be considered an institution. Yet for all our complaining and desire to overturn these institutions, we often don't understand why they came about in the first place.

Institutions form out of love and freedom. We see this best in the micro-institution of the family. I was recently scrolling through Instagram and saw a side-by-side image posted by a friend. In the first photo, she was in the arms of her husband and wearing a wedding dress. The second photo was taken in the same field, only this time, they were both in regular clothes, each holding a child. In their wild, free, romantic love for each other, they did the craziest thing imaginable: they pledged their undying love to each other under the authority of God, the Church, and the government, and then had some kids. Out of extraordinary love, they became a family.

It is the same with the Catholic Church. Jesus Christ came to set us free. Out of his insane love for us, he set up a way for that love to be offered to every single individual on earth throughout every age. The Church exists as a way for us to live in the freedom that Christ delivered to us on the Cross.

The apostles, with crazy love for their Savior, responded to Jesus by continuing the Church that he established to the best of their ability. Think about just how committed these men and women were to spreading the Gospel. They were so on fire that at one point, they converted three thousand people in one day (see Acts 2:41). They walked around performing miracles and casting out demons in the name of Jesus Christ. They traveled all over the ancient world at great personal peril to bring this new message of Jesus Christ to all people. It was the apostles, in their wild love for God, who were the first to live out the hierarchy of the Church to provide order. They set up the role of priests, deacons, and elders to take care of the faithful and guard the Church from heresy. Out of their prayer, and the instructions of our Savior, we participate in the sacraments. It was all born in love, out of the desire to bring every heart that would ever exist to know Jesus and make him known.

Comfortingly, and heartbreakingly, if we were to blow it all up today, those who are in love with Jesus would eventually re-create a church with similar problems. We can see proof of this in the Protestant Reformation. Martin Luther broke away from the very corrupt Catholic Church at the time only to make another institution with different rules and, eventually, the same corruption. Today, there are more than forty thousand Christian denominations,[4] all of them with a different system of authority, different rules, and the same corruption problems, scaled to the size of their church. This in no way excuses the atrocities committed in our house. The point is that institutions are created out of love and corrupted out of sin every time. The answer isn't to get rid of the institution; it is to get rid of the sin. Only then will these institutions, whether family, government, church, or other, serve people with the purpose for which they were made.

The Scriptural Basis for the Priesthood

Since I was a teenager, I've known that Jesus, in Matthew 16:18, gave Peter the keys to the kingdom, and that made him the first pope. Peter is the "rock" upon which Jesus built his Church. But I always wondered, *Is that it?* We get this whole Church from one cryptic verse in scripture? From there, we get the cardinals in red hats, the bishops with their miters, and the priests, men in black? I'm not sure if you ever learned about that scripture verse in Matthew 16, but there is more there than meets the eye, and it has everything to do with how we read the Bible.

A few weeks before I learned how to greet the pope in etiquette class, I took a scripture class with Jeff Cavins, a Methodist pastor turned Catholic and Bible scholar. I sat in his class, eyes full of awe and wonder, as he explained how the scriptures are woven together: Jesus is the center of everything. The Old Testament reveals the New Testament, and the New Testament brings fulfillment to the promises of the Old. He explained the verses in which Jesus gives Peter the keys to the kingdom as it relates to the Davidic kingdom in the Old Testament, and I was able to understand the priesthood with a whole new meaning. Here is what he said.

Cavins reminded us that in Matthew 16, Jesus with his apostles and Peter has just affirmed Jesus as the Messiah. As we discussed earlier, Jesus tells Peter he is the rock upon which Jesus will build his Church. Jesus says to Peter, "I will give you the keys of the kingdom of heaven, and whatever you bind on earth shall be bound in heaven, and whatever you loose on earth shall be loosed in heaven" (19).

Thousands of years before that moment, during the time of the prophet Isaiah, the God of Israel set up a kingdom for his people. At the time of King David's rule, God established the role of a "prime minister" whose job was to run the kingdom while the king was away. The office is described in Isaiah 22:20–22:

> In that day I will call my servant Eliakim the son of Hilkiah, and I will clothe him with your robe, and will bind your girdle on him, and will commit your authority to his hand; and he shall be a father to the inhabitants of Jerusalem and to the house of Judah. I will place on his shoulder the key of the house of David; he shall open, and none shall shut; and he shall shut, and none shall open.

Cavins pointed out that Jesus' language to Peter parallels that of Isaiah almost exactly. As Jesus came to fulfill the Old Covenant, he also meant to set up a kingdom. The Jews of Jesus' time would have interpreted this exchange in light of the words of Isaiah: Jesus was setting up the office of "prime minister" for the new covenant. This is currently the role of the pope. His entire job is to lead the Church in faithfulness to Jesus Christ and his teachings until he returns.

I walked out of class that day with my brain on the floor. I had learned something incredible. I learned that God had a plan to set up the Catholic Church since the beginning. It wasn't an afterthought or a consequence. It was a plan. All of our popes, bishops, and priests have been called by God to be part of this Gospel machine.

Unfortunately, the foundation in Christ doesn't mean that those who accept leadership positions are perfect. They aren't and never were. Just as the kingdom of Israel rarely enjoyed good and noble leaders, so too has the Church seen many corrupt men lead it throughout history.

Jesus sees the deceit and corruption in our hearts, and he saw just how awful the religious leaders of his day could be, and yet he chose to establish his Church on earth. He chose imperfect men to lead imperfect people and show us that imperfect men can become saints, and so can we. He gave us mercy, forgiveness, and the presence of the Holy Spirit to balance the scales, and then he promised that the gates of hell would never prevail against the Church.

This last part, by the way, is the best, and it has been a source of consolation for me throughout the recent scandals. Jesus never said that it wouldn't *feel* as if the gates of hell were prevailing; he said they wouldn't. Keep in mind that Jesus was dead and yet he defeated death; he fulfilled his promise when it looked as if all was lost. When Christ returns, victory will be claimed and justice will be granted to every person ever hurt by those who were supposed to be the face of Christ and abused their position. The institution, created out of love and perpetuated by imperfect men, will be brought to perfection in the end.

Treasures in Clay: The Humanity of the Priest

I am currently re-listening to the autobiography of Archbishop Fulton Sheen, *Treasure in Clay*. Archbishop Sheen was a television sensation in the 1950s and won an Emmy for his show, *Life Is Worth Living*. He was the auxiliary bishop of New York and eventually became the bishop of Rochester. Sheen was fiercely holy, not perfect, but a model for all priests to follow in how he loved God, understood his priesthood, lived out his vocation, and boldly loved others. His book is on Audible, and most of his shows are on YouTube if you want to treat yourself and get to know this man before he becomes a saint.

At the beginning of his autobiography, he explains why he titled the book *Treasure in Clay*. The vocation to the priesthood, he says, is a treasure—holy, given by God from heaven. It resides, though, within imperfect humans, the clay. Thus every priest is fostering the treasure of his vocation within the clay of his humanity. This is a beautiful description of vocation for anyone; God, who is perfect, calls us, and we live out that call within the imperfection of our humanity. Priests must live out the high call of being Jesus Christ to his people, and they have to answer this call amid their brokenness. Over the years of meeting priests and spending time with many of them up close, I have seen just how deeply they need our understanding, prayers, and friendship.

Men and women who enter religious life are the products of the same culture we are. They are not perfect porcelain dolls on pedestals—they come with pasts and egos and darkness and sexual brokenness. They are dealing with the effects of those things as they try to become salt and light to the world. And yes, they should constantly strive to be worthy of the call that the Lord has placed in their lives. The Holy Spirit makes this possible, and no past sin is an excuse to avoid this call.

I have worked at a parish with priests. I have sat and visited with priests over drinks or coffee. I have seen small details of their jobs and have noticed that on a practical level, we often don't set them up for success. A priest in charge of the parish ministry and business usually has very little training on how to deal with the latter, which means the parish business side will be neglected, poorly run, or completely outsourced. Often, he lives alone in the rectory, maybe with one or two other priests who don't spend any time building a relationship with one another.

What effect will this type of setup have on any person? First, if there are no checks and balances when it comes to running the parish, the priest can either feel quickly defeated with all there is to do or give in to his ego as the sole decision maker with underpaid church workers to do his bidding. Neither is good. If he is in charge of finances, something he may know little about, there is a good chance he will mismanage church funds. If he is constantly engaged in serving his parishioners by celebrating Mass, administering the sacraments, visiting the hospitals, and officiating at funerals, it can be easy for a priest to burn out. If he has no accountability, no relationships to challenge him to continue to become holy, and no personal support, temptation is even harder to resist. Before he knows it, the priest can be living in some secret scandal. This is not the story of every priest, but I have seen over the years that the way we view people in religious life does not give them the grace of their humanity or challenge them to continue to be faithful to their vocation.

In the end, the reputation of the Church does not rely on the actions of only the clergy. It must rely on all of us. We have received a treasure from God to develop in the clay of our brokenness. That treasure, that call from God, is for each one of us to become a saint. For too many years now, laypeople have thought that we can never be as holy as those in religious life. God has never made that distinction. Pope John Paul II recognized this in his encyclical about the mission of the Church, *Lumen Gentium*: "The classes and duties of life are many, but holiness is one" (41). Our paths to holiness look different, but the end is holiness nonetheless.

The unbelievable corruption that exists within the leadership of the Catholic Church reveals the face of evil, but so does the scandalous complacency and blandly sinister lack of belief of those who are in the pews. If ordinary Catholic men and women weren't so enamored with the glamour of the world, maybe we would have seen and been able to help correct the course of our brothers in the priesthood earlier. It is an even bigger scandal that millions of people are "nominal Catholics." Yes, it is more damaging to see the hypocrisy revealed in those who have used the institution of the Church to chase their love of the world. The priesthood needs to be held accountable. And bad priests need to be taken out of ministry. We need our priests to become shepherds again who will fight for their sheep. As infuriating as it is, I have learned that the abuse scandal is a call for me to examine my failings and hypocrisies. Maybe it's also time for laypeople to examine our consciences and become the Catholics we are called to be.

Why I Stayed

I was three months into my missionary year at the University of Tennessee, and my zeal was running dry. I didn't want to pray. I was driving to my scheduled holy hour with complete dread. Another day of prayer. Another day of pursuing students who were fighting their own battles and might stand me up for that coffee date again. I was tired. The poverty I had so valiantly chosen to live as a missionary sucked. On this day, I had had enough.

I drove into the parking lot, walked into the chapel, and sat down—my heart was as dry as the Sahara. I held nothing back as I told the Lord every detail of how I felt. I told him I didn't want to do this anymore; I'd rather go on vacation, go shopping, or really be doing anything else. I received no response from the Lord, just silence, but then eventually peace.

As my anger faded, I came to a sobering realization. Let's say I got what I wanted that day. I walked out of the chapel, packed my bags, and went on vacation. Let's say I took a break from Christianity altogether and just drank in the pleasures of the world. Let's say I had all the money I wanted. Once I tired of drinking mai tais, shopping, and superficial entertainment, where would I go? What would I do? I asked myself this question, and the answer hit me like a two-by-four. I had known it all along. I would end up finding a chapel and falling on my face before my Lord in the Eucharist. I would run from the chapel, only to run back. Only here was the Truth, the full presence of the Word Made Flesh. Here was the love for which I was made. If I walked away, I would have to walk back.

For years now, I have called this moment in the chapel my "Peter moment." Perhaps you remember that moment I described in the Gospel of John, right after Jesus has proclaimed he is the bread of life. Many of Christ's disciples stopped following him because this statement was so shocking and challenging. Jesus then turned to his apostles, the twelve who were most faithful, and asked, "Will you also go away?" Peter responded, "Lord, to whom shall we go? You have the words of eternal life; and we have believed, and have come to know, that you are the Holy One of God" (Jn 6:67–69).

Even if Peter wanted to leave, he knew he would have to return because he had come to know that Jesus is the Christ. If you have found the Son of God, the Savior, the image of the invisible God, the search has to stop. We know in our being when we have found what we have been longing for. That day in the chapel, I had to say the same thing to God. No, I didn't want to be there, but to whom should I go to fill the depth of longing in my heart? To whom should I go to reveal to me the truth of this life and the next? To whom should I go for redemption, and the revelation of all the beauty that is offered us in joy and suffering in this life? I have found the one for whom my soul longs, and I must stay with him no matter what.

In the midst of hearing about all the abuse scandals, I told my husband that I wished I could leave the Church. It feels as if the Catholic Church doesn't deserve my loyalty when there are wolves disguised as shepherds who are making it difficult for all of the faithful men and women, hearts on fire, to bring about revival. It would be so nice to head down the road and belong to another Christian church that doesn't face this problem. I believe that Jesus is present in these churches, and I believe that the Holy Spirit is blessing them in powerful ways. Jesus, however, prayed that we would be one Church. Jesus did not pray that we would be one if and only if that Church stayed pure. He was the Son of God, not an idiot, and he knew the heart of humanity far better than the rest of us. The Church has had problems since the beginning, and so has every denomination that has splintered off of it. If I believe Catholicism can bring me as close to the fullness of Truth in this life as possible, and if I believe true faithfulness to the teachings of the Church turns ordinary people into saints, then honestly, to where shall I go? I would leave, feel good for a while, and then have to return home to the Church that holds the crucifix, the Eucharist, the sacraments, and the saints.

A friend of mine told me she sat with a religious sister and asked her what she thought of the scandals. They discussed how so much had gone on for so many years that it was both horrifying and mind-boggling. After the discussion, the holy sister looked at the top of the door where a crucifix hung. She said, "I am just glad I know. For too many years, our Lord has carried this burden alone."

Friend, I share in all your emotions when it comes to these scandals. The pain is real and, in many ways, irreversible. That's the problem with evil. Evil itself never leads to good. Only God in his perfect goodness can draw good out of evil.

On the other hand, I have seen signs for great hope. The men and women I know right now who are entering religious life are doing so overwhelmingly for the right reasons. They love the Lord and are committed to loving God and his Church. My hope for you is that you would not just walk away or celebrate that you left years ago. I hope that you would not write off Catholicism because of broken men who chose not follow its teachings. I hope that instead, you will struggle with this issue and search out your own heart for loyalty. What is evil in the institution, and what is it in your own heart? Can God's grace cover both? Is it okay to use the sin of another to excuse us from our call to holiness? Is the Church the fullness of Truth? If not, where is that Truth? If so, then we must soberly say "To whom shall we go?" and stay to fight for renewal in the Church of our Savior.

6.
Sorting Out the Heart of *Sexuality

What I Experienced

I love musicals. Just this morning, I performed "This Is Me" from *The Greatest Showman* for my daughters as we ate breakfast. There is something about breaking into a powerful song about everyday life that reminds me life is more than a series of actions to be completed. Moments were meant to bring us into a sense of wonder, and musicals accentuate the wonder and gravity of everyday life.

You can imagine, then, how excited I was to finally see *Spring Awakening* several years ago. My friend Christina and I got dressed up in our fancy clothes and headed to the theater for our big night. I had no idea what the play was about but learned quickly in the first act that this was a story of teenagers discovering their sexuality. I was surprised, but shouldn't have been. After all, isn't everything about sexual discovery these days?

The play opens with a young woman, Wendla Bergmann, asking her mother to explain where babies come from. She is entering into puberty, but her mother will not give her a decent explanation of reproduction. Instead, her mother simply tells Wendla that in order to have a baby, a woman must love her husband with all her heart. After this conversation, the musical takes us to her school where we quickly find out that none of the young women in the town have been given any useful, truthful information about their sexuality. The young men, meanwhile, are having similar discussions because one of them is having erotic dreams. Melchior Gabor, the male protagonist, is an atheist and the only character that has a decent understanding of sexuality, which he only got from reading books. The adults in the play are judgmental, secretive, and manipulative, which creates an environment of fear and repression among the students. Slowly, the audience learns that the characters in the play are living in an environment of abuse and disorder, disguised as a good Christian town. This all comes to a head as the first act crescendos and Wendla and Melchior end up having sex in a hayloft.

The second act descends further down a dark hole of chaos and tragedy. One of the students kills himself, and the murder is blamed on Melchior. Wendla finds out that she is pregnant and freaks out because she didn't know that sex could lead to a baby. Her mother is unapologetic and schedules an abortion for her despite their Christianity. In the end, Wendla dies of a botched abortion and Melchior tries to kill himself with a razor when he hears of Wendla's death. He changes his mind when the spirits of Wendla and Moritz (another character) appear and convince Melchior to move on. Devastating. I seriously walked out with a tragedy hangover. This was pure Shakespearean tragedy with all the hope of nihilism: no warm fuzzies, no joy, and no turn of events in which the hero finds in himself the strength to carry on.

I didn't like the play. I didn't like that the smartest guy in the room was an atheist, further supporting the idea that those who believe in God are idiots (not true). I didn't like that Christianity was portrayed as so messed up on sexual teaching—but I understood why. In many ways, the Church at large, including the

Catholic Church, has earned the reputation that it either hates sex and all it entails or knows very little about it. The Church has not fostered a culture that supports open, honest, educated, and compassionate conversations on sexuality. Most Catholic churchgoers instead learn about sexuality from the culture at large and have very little understanding how to live out their sexuality well.

I am in no way an expert on sexuality. As part of this millennial generation though, I witnessed all of my friends, myself included, struggle to make sense of their own sexuality and how it fits into religion. I have then watched them reject the religion part and go their own way. I have watched my generation make terrible mistakes due to misunderstanding the purpose of sexuality. Along with them, I have stood in front of the mirror wrapped in shame. I have winced away from painful memories, wishing they did not exist and that I hadn't made the choices I did. The misuse and misunderstanding of sex is a major cause of pain and suffering in our society, and I could never write to you honestly if I didn't address it.

The best I can remember is that my classmates and I started to learn about sex at our Catholic school in seventh grade. I knew very little about sex at all but of course knew it was something to be saved for marriage. I have two vivid memories from my first sex ed class. In the first, my teacher chewed up an Oreo and spit it onto a napkin. She then offered it to a guy in the first row. He of course turned it down. The point to this demonstration? After you had sex outside of marriage, no one would want you; you would be irreparably damaged. The second memory also includes a demonstration: My teacher put tape on her arm and ripped it off. We then all took turns trying to stick the tape to our arm until the tape was no longer sticky at all. The point here? Sex with multiple people decreases your ability to bond. The more sex you had with different partners, the less able you would be to connect with each partner.

The next year I moved to the high school for eighth grade, and over the next few years we would participate in the "abstinence program" every year. My classmates and I learned how sex organs worked from our teachers, and guest speakers such as doctors and youth ministers spoke to us on other sexual topics. We learned a ton of statistics and saw graphic pictures of sexually transmitted diseases. We watched videos of chastity speakers and even had the very young Jason Evert, now a Catholic chastity rock star, speak at our school.

Looking back, I would give my school a B in sex education, especially after meeting so many people in my twenties who were having plenty of sex but knew nothing about it. I can honestly say that I walked out of high school with a real understanding of the male and female bodies, as well as the physical and emotional consequences of sex, which is more than many my age can say. I can also say that my elementary school and my high school were trying to be faithful to the Church's teachings on love and sex. At the time, I personally thought that the Oreo and tape demonstration made good points, but as I listened to others joke about STDs and make fun of our teachers, it was clear that most of us who had gone through the abstinence program would be practicing anything but abstinence.

Looking back after years of mistakes, I now see where my Catholic school sex ed went wrong: it came from a place of fear. I get it, I have three little girls now, and there is some really bad stuff out there. As a parent, the steel Everlast chastity belt worn by Maid Marian in *Robin Hood: Men in Tights* sounds like a pretty good idea. My classmates and I were given accurate information, but it was presented with the understanding that we were permanently damaged if we didn't get married as virgins and that if we did have sex out of wedlock we were definitely going to get a fatal venereal disease. My Catholic sex ed painted the world of sexuality as scary and depressing. There are definitely elements of truth in all of this. Once virginity is lost, that virginity cannot be regained. Sex outside of marriage can definitely lead to inconvenient, permanent, or downright fatal diseases. The misuse of sexuality very often leads people into dark places. The problem is that while fear can be a great motivator, it is many times only temporary. Very few people love God because they are afraid of hell. We should fear hell. We should not want to go there, but it shouldn't be the main reason we serve the Lord. Love should be the reason.

Furthermore, the undertones of fear in our education didn't match the invitations presented to us by the culture. Everywhere we looked, sex was painted as fun and fulfilling. I was in sixth grade when the movie *American Pie* came out, a movie about a high schooler's quest to lose his virginity. That same year Christina Aguilera, age sixteen, released her song "Genie in a Bottle." My husband and I now marvel at how unbelievably sexual that song really is, and I was singing it all the time as a sixth grader. The message about sex from the culture was and is that virgins are stupid, sex is no big deal, and once you have it your life will be better. You will find love, fun, and increased social status. When the message of fear from our Church collides with the message from our culture, which do you think will win the hearts of pubescent, hormonal teenagers?

As represented in *Spring Awakening*, Christians in general are seen as repressive when it comes to sex, and in many ways the Church has earned this reputation. For too many years, young Christians have received little real education from their parents or the Church besides "Don't do it before marriage." Sex is not traditionally talked about in Christian circles, and for years, at least in the Catholic Church, the way it was taught sent the message that sex was only for making babies. No fun, just babies.

Most of us have heard of a young unmarried Catholic woman who got pregnant. She was sent away, shamed by a very judgmental congregation, or was forced into a secret abortion as was Wendla in *Spring Awakening*. In fact, I have worked for women's organizations that produce small-group study guides specifically for women in the Church who are experiencing unplanned pregnancy. Many of these women feel they must get an abortion rather than let anyone in the Church know that they got pregnant.

I bet many of us watched a friend struggle secretly with their homosexuality while attending Bible studies. Without even thinking deeply, I can count eight of my peers who were involved in Church, came out of the closet, and then left the Church. They felt as if there was no place for them in the house of God if they weren't heterosexual, and far too often, we in the pews have been complicit in fostering this message. In my own walk with Jesus, the Church's stance on homosexuality has been one of the hardest for me to navigate. Seeing my dear friends leave one by one because they believe the Church sees them as bad is heartbreaking.

So for generations now, the Catholic Church has seemed to yell one gigantic no when it comes to sex. No sex outside of marriage. No sex for fun. No contraception. No homosexuality. No mistakes. No mercy. It seems as though the culture is one big yes to sex and therefore love, while the Church's repeated no is also a no to love. To make matters worse, many in the hierarchy of the Christian Church, Catholic and Protestant, have created a convoluted mess of evil hypocrisy when it comes to sex. As we discussed in the last chapter, the sexual abuse and secret prostitutes that have been revealed in scandal after scandal is infuriating and disgusting to laypeople who for years have been expected to pray, pay, and obey. The Church, like the contemporary culture, has not always provided a clear path when it comes to navigating teachings on sexuality.

With so much confusion, so many mixed messages, and so much hypocrisy, it makes sense that the many people who aren't heterosexual or don't want to reserve sex for marriage would walk away from the Church. If the Church truly is a gigantic billboard of no to sex, then millions of people have left for very good reasons.

What I Learned

Right after college graduation, I spent five weeks on mission in Prague, Czech Republic. It was in Prague that the Lord started bringing me into the depths of my heart to work out the darkness, and in that process I heard the first faint inklings of a call to full-time ministry. I had already accepted a job offer, though, and after the summer I needed to be in San Jose for three weeks of training in internal audit at PricewaterhouseCoopers. With a heart excited for the future and in love with Jesus Christ, I packed my bags, dreaming of my first real paycheck.

I entered into training with twentysomethings from around the nation who were ready to work insane hours for a chance to find a pot of gold at the end of the corporate ladder. Having just returned from Prague, I was on fire for Jesus and ready to share the Gospel with anyone who would listen. Among my peers, with whom I had a great time, I quickly became known as "the Christian girl who was a total prude but could still hang."

On the last day of our training, I went to lunch with some of my fellow trainees. As we were sitting at the table, the topic of conversation turned to hookups. I can't quite remember the context of the conversation, but I will never forget one specific part. I turned toward one of the guys and said, "Here's the deal: you will always have the upper hand when it comes to sex. No matter how strong or sexually driven a woman is, she will be left with some kind of heartache, even if she doesn't recognize it. Because sex is physical for you, you can walk away from a casual hookup almost completely unscathed." His tone was upbeat, almost optimistic, as he agreed with me: "Oh, yeah, you are totally right. Honestly, I feel bad for a lot of the girls I hook up with because I know it's harder for them than it is for me."

It was as if he had opened his mouth and the bluntest of truths just fell out. Over the three weeks that I had gotten to know this guy, he seemed nice enough. I don't think he meant any harm to anyone, but he was taught about sex by a culture that says anything goes.

That conversation made a deep impression on me. Even if there is only a tiny part of our soul that still recognizes Truth, it is there and sometimes we hear it. We know that the promises of cheap sex are nothing but cheap lies, and we know the consequences, but we are so resistant to anything that would tell us to restrict our behavior for the sake of something better. My friend that day was only half right in what he admitted. After years of making my own mistakes, I saw that there was no way whatsoever for me to enter into a casual sexual experience and emerge with zero baggage. Eventually, I started to see that no one leaves a sexual encounter free and clear. Ever. A sexual experience for a man may be "less emotional," but poor decisions always have emotional consequences. If the goal of this life is to become virtuous, to become a good human being, a man's misuse of sex will keep him from ever attaining such nobility. Perpetual use of another person leads to self-abuse and self-deception. The deceived soul can never find true freedom. The truth is ours for the taking, and by the time I became a young adult, it was easy to see. But having turned away from any traditional upbringing, I had to fight my way back to what I, in my being, knew.

My Journey

By the time I was a senior in high school, I was starting to notice inconsistencies between what I was learning about the world in church and what I was seeing in the world with my own eyes. This was especially true with sexuality. My friends had their first sexual encounters, and I saw different outcomes from those our Catholic school's abstinence program predicted. People were having sex, and their lives weren't being ruined. They seemed fine. It wasn't like the movies in which the clouds part and true love abounds forever in a childless rollercoaster of eternal romance, but people weren't turning into zombies either. It seemed to me there was a middle ground. Hell didn't swallow you whole if you had sex outside of marriage; it was just part of life.

As I was trying to make sense of what I heard in church and what I saw unfolding before me, I also discovered half the members of my youth group were hooking up with one another on the side. I had been attracted to the youth group because earlier members had modeled a life of deep love for the Lord, but the current members said one thing and lived another.

Watching my friends lose their virginity with no visible earth-shattering consequences and seeing the sexual hypocrisy of my youth group friends left me caring less and less about my faith. The icing on the cake, however, was that I started dating my first "real" and also "worst ever" boyfriend. Obsession with another person will drive you to compromise every single thing you hold dear, as it did with me. This was the recipe for the unraveling of my childhood faith. It didn't happen right away, but those religious rules eventually drove me to an ultimatum. Did I believe enough to follow or not? My answer would eventually be that I didn't really believe.

So I walked into college with merely remnants of my belief in the Lord, a deep desire to drink deeply of American culture, a deep desire to be loved, and an indifferent attitude toward sex before marriage. At this point, you may be expecting me to tell you that I went off the deep end. You may be waiting for me to tell you that I was highly promiscuous and ended up with an STD or pregnancy. Though I know plenty of people who ended up dealing with those consequences, none of that happened to me. I dabbled in the hookup culture with relatively few sexual experiences throughout college, but it was enough. It was devastating for me. I don't mean devastating in the sense that I was completely destroyed and on the ground crying every time I chose to hook up. What I do mean is that over four years I slowly numbed my heart and degraded my self-worth. Though few and somewhat far between, I was well aware that these guys I was hooking up with did not love me. I was well aware that I was using them as much as they were using me, searching for an experience of euphoria that I never found.

Thankfully, I could only ignore this reality for so long. I eventually recognized the effects of my life in the mirror and saw the fatigue of my soul in my eyes. I didn't quite know why I was hooking up, but I knew that if I hadn't found love with this sort of behavior already, I would never find it. I knew I was a shadow of the woman I was meant to be, and I also knew that part of the problem was cynicism in my heart from years of somewhat sparse, definitely meaningless, degrading hookup encounters with men who did not care for me. I knew I needed to make some changes, and hooking up with someone I didn't love was now off the table. I wasn't swearing off sex until marriage at this point, but I was swearing off anything of the sort until I was in a committed, loving relationship. Thanks be to God, that relationship didn't come until I had accepted the Church's teaching on love and marriage.

Remembering the Church's "repressive" teachings on sexuality, I started opening my heart to more traditional teachings on sex as I very slowly made my way back to Christianity. It's not that I never made mistakes after that—I did—but I was striving for something better and I was learning. The more I learned, the more I was able to pick myself back up and step onto the path of virtue.

Finding Freedom in the Church's Teaching on Sexuality

After willfully taking myself out of the dating scene in my early twenties, I became a cultural observer. I would go out with my friends, have a drink, dance, and then watch the social interactions unfold before my eyes; I started to notice that my story was not unique. Sexual experiences outside of marriage weren't just bad for me; they seemed to be bad for all of my friends as well. I remember a dear friend of mine who would hook up with men pretty freely. She often talked about engaging in sex with total detachment from any sort of real relationship. She said it was empowering to be able to have sex with no strings attached. I wanted to believe her, but I saw that every time one of these "casual" hookups stopped calling, she would stay in bed all day.

I watched another friend prolong a toxic relationship because they had started having sex. She had wanted to wait until marriage before she had sex again—he talked her out of it, and she wasted her time trying to make that doomed relationship work. I saw my friends contract embarrassing, inconvenient, and dangerous STDs. I saw my guy friends become caricatures of the men they were made to be. As I watched the way they talked and treated women, I saw selfish toddlers emerge from grown men's bodies. All in all, I never watched a friend of mine emerge from an extramarital sexual experience with a deeper sense of self-worth, with a higher sense of security, or having become a better person because of it. Yes, I have friends who fell in love and married each other despite having sex before marriage, but again, I never saw in them a higher virtue because of it—I would contend that they found a deeper love in spite of it. Underneath the shiny surface of extramarital sex lurked a cynical, slow destruction.

I started to see that the Church, with all its flawed methods of teaching on sex, had tried to pass on to me and my peers an understanding of sex that was much closer to the reality. Sex is powerful. If it wasn't, we wouldn't see such deep wounds manifest from its misuse or abuse. The Church calls us to reserve sex for marriage because it is only within marriage that sex can be safe.

It is only a marriage that can properly hold and foster the sexual union. Although priests, teachers, youth ministers, and catechists have often made us think of chastity as a scary, unfun world to be avoided at all costs, when I finally read the Church's official definition, I was blown away by its straightforward simplicity.

> Chastity means the *successful integration of sexuality within the person* and thus the inner unity of man in his bodily and spiritual being. Sexuality, in which man's belonging to the bodily and biological world is expressed, becomes personal and truly human when it is integrated into the relationship of one person to another, in the complete and lifelong mutual gift of a man and a woman. The virtue of chastity therefore involves the integrity of the person and the integrality of the gift. (*CCC*, 2337; emphasis added)

The Oreo and tape demonstrations gave us a skewed vision of chastity. Sexuality is not our total identity, consuming everything about us, but it is also not nothing. We are not completely irredeemable if we make mistakes with sex, and we can cause major damage to ourselves because of sex's power. Sex is meant to be handled with care, to be ordered, to dwell in its proper place.

That proper place in the person and in society, whether we like it or not, is marriage. Why? Because sex is unitive and procreative. Both of these things are permanent. Sex permanently unites us to our partner. The *Catechism of the Catholic Church* tells us that sex is not simply biological; it concerns the innermost being of the human person.[1] If the sexual act results in a child, that child is a tangible, separate, permanent life that requires the care of permanent love. The consequences of sex are permanent and therefore must be held by something that is permanent. It really is that straightforward and simple. It may not be easy, and we may not like it, but that doesn't change it.

I started to discover these teachings by reading John Paul II's Theology of the Body, listening to well-spoken priests and pastors, and reflecting on my own experiences. I started to embrace them from the inside out, and I noticed something start to happen in my life: many of my self-esteem issues started to fade away—not all of them, but many of them. I noticed that my interests started to change. I spent less time worrying about impressing guys or how I was going to get a boyfriend and more time reading, creating, and learning. I developed more genuine friendships with men because I knew we would not be taking our relationship any further than it was meant to be taken. I was also able to discern the type of men with whom I would spend my time because I could more easily see their motivations. The more I sought to live out the Church's teachings on sexuality, the healthier I found myself becoming in my own skin and the easier I found it to chase after wisdom. I was no longer compelled to participate in hookup culture. The Church, in passing down the wisdom of the Gospel of Jesus Christ, revealed that sex is good and worth the wait. No gimmicks, no compromises.

St. Paul tells us in Galatians 5:1, "For freedom Christ has set us free; stand fast therefore, and do not submit again to a yoke of slavery." By walking away from the Church's teachings on sexuality, I had enslaved myself to hookup culture. I had rejected the freedom offered to me in Christ and bound myself to the culture's favorite false idol: misused, self-seeking sexuality. No, I don't always want to follow these teachings perfectly. They are simple, but they are not easy. Yet in following them, I have attained a life not of perfection but of joy, and in the end, it is joy we are all after.

Why I Stayed

During the year I was a youth minister in Tampa, we took our students to the Holocaust Memorial Museum in Washington, D.C. I read *The Diary of Anne Frank* at a very young age and have always been interested in anything dealing with World War II. As we were walking through this memorial to one of the darkest times in human history, I came across a heartening caption about the Catholic Church.

I was reading through the history of Jewish persecution in Germany before it turned into full-blown extermination. The plaque at which I stood told the story of Hitler's slow, then fast, removal of the rights of Germany's Jewish citizens. First he marked them, then he separated them from other Germans, and then he took away their ability to participate in society. Eventually the Nazis removed them from their homes and gathered them in ghettos, and before long, even worse horrors began to unfold.

As I read through the story at the museum, I read about how the Catholic Church and other Christian churches were complicit with Germany in this slow persecution. Too many church leaders compromised the Truth, hoping to protect their own interests by not angering the Nazis. As I kept reading, however, I saw many examples of ordinary Catholics who stood by the Truth and tried to protect their Jewish brothers and sisters. History is kinder to those who live out the Truth for better or worse.

Pride welled up within me. Here, immortalized for onlookers to see, was the testimony of history that men and women shine when they choose to stand for Truth even when it is hard. There is no doubt we have failed miserably to honor the tenets of the Gospel of Jesus Christ in practice throughout history. We are a Church for sinners, led by sinners. Yet our teachings are holy. When we follow them, we become holy. Here, before me, in the midst of such horror, was an example of what the Church should be: holy, standing for freedom at all times, and completely uncompromising.

At this time in my life, I was also revisiting the Church's teachings on sexuality as I was figuring out what it means to be Catholic. As I read through the Church's teaching on sex and marriage, I saw the same trend. Every other Christian church has softened its teachings on sexuality, molding itself in some form to fit the culture. But the Catholic Church has stood firm. This hasn't necessarily been the reality in individual Catholic practice, as we have discussed at length, but the truth at the heart is still the same. This discovery allowed me to trust the Church as an authority in my life. I noticed that where the Church has stood firm, Truth seemed to reign, and those who actually followed this authority, although they are few and far between, seemed to have a deeper joy than the rest of society.

For years, I justified my choices in pursuit of my passions. I thought I was seeking happiness, but in the end I was anything but happy. Psalm 1:6 says, "For the LORD knows the way of the righteous, but the way of the wicked will perish." Left to our own devices, we will most likely make a mess of our lives. How often do we try to clean up the disasters in our lives that started with good intentions, only to make things worse? This is especially true when it comes to sexual wounds.

I have seen in myself over the years that often I am my own worst enemy. I am the common denominator in all of my messes. I need a firm, sound teaching on which to stand that will lead me from death to life. I need to find an authority that won't fold when I don't necessarily like that it requires more than my sinful desires. This is why I submit to the Church's teaching on sexuality. When I weigh the scales, our culture is far too wounded to be right on this issue, and our Church has turned out countless holy individuals throughout history. Those who stay in the Church but who don't follow its teachings end up falling into the mess.

My friend, I have no idea where you stand when it comes to the Church's teachings on sexuality. Wherever you are, I invite you to take inventory of your own life and those around you. What was your experience? Do you think it is worth revisiting? Think of the people in your life who are doing whatever is right in their own eyes according to their sexuality. Do they seem fulfilled? Do they seem healthy in body and spirit? Do they seem well balanced? What about you? Where do you land in the midst of it all? Could you be more free? Could you be more ordered within? Have you been able to accomplish this on your own?

I firmly believe we can love Jesus with all of our heart and still never live in true freedom if we do not embrace chastity. Jesus has broken the chains of bondage for us, and the teachings of his Church, especially those on sexuality, keep us from submitting again to the yoke of slavery. My hope for you is that you can forgive those in the Church who have muddied the waters on chastity in one way or another. I pray you will decide it is worth it to present yourself moldable to God Almighty, so he can create the order of his glory within you. My hope is that you would allow him to bind up your wounds so our society looks at you and sees a crown of glory on your life that faintly reveals the scars of the thorns of sin. Sin should never have the last word. Take another look at the Church's teaching on sexuality. Wrestle with it, ask the questions, and be willing to be wrong. You may find the freedom to be had on the other side.

7.

Digging into "Backward" Teachings

What I Experienced

It was time for my afternoon coffee. My rule is one in the morning, and one in the afternoon, no more, sometimes less. I packed up my backpack and closed my Bible as I headed toward Starbucks. I'd had plans with my FOCUS missionary teammate, Andrea, but she had gone home sick. Disappointed at the change in plans, I asked God to let me meet someone during my break so I could share his love and make new friends.

As I waited in the Starbucks line, I noticed that the young man behind me was dressed well. His shoes looked very expensive and matched his outfit perfectly. Unable to resist, I complimented his outfit and fashion sense, and we struck up a conversation. The line was long, which gave us plenty of time to get acquainted before we ordered our coffee. By the time we reached the front, I had learned that he was not a student at the university but was in town visiting his boyfriend. He learned I was a Catholic missionary who had only been living in the city for six months. Knowing the Catholic Church has a reputation for being "against homosexuality," he could have easily said goodbye to me and gone on his way, but we clicked. He was waiting for his boyfriend, and I had an hour to kill. We grabbed our coffees and walked around the campus for a while. The Lord had given me a friend.

We shared a ton of interests, and he listened as I told him about the life I had chosen in service to Jesus. I don't remember all the details of our conversation. I do remember, however, that many of his stories were sad, as he told of being a drifter raised in the Bible Belt. At the end of our time together, we sat on the curb, our after-noon coffees now gone, and I told him about God's love for him. As I spoke, this young man who grew up in the Bible Belt hung on my every word. It may not have been the first time someone told him that God loved him, but it must have been a long time because he clearly needed to hear it. According to him, he had chosen a lifestyle that was incompatible with the Christian God. He decided that a man like him didn't belong in church. This prodigal son didn't understand that the God of mercy was continually watching for his return, ready to open his arms to him, in his mess and brokenness. We prayed together and parted ways, he toward his boyfriend, me toward my religion.

As I walked away, I thought of my many friends who struggle with same-sex attraction. I thought of what I witnessed them go through, and I started to pray for them all. I have watched many of my friends, even my best friends, come out of the closet. All of them struggled to reconcile their religious upbringing, to which they have some sort of allegiance, and their sexual desires. Typical-ly, after a couple of years of telling almost no one about their inner battle, they finally make the courageous choice to be honest with their friends and family about their struggles. Within six months, they are usually gone from the Church, as they do not trust the Christian Church to be a haven in which they can figure it all out. Before the Lord can even work in their hearts, some self-righteous church person spouts out Church teaching with little regard for the individual's experience or internal struggle. The strugglers perceive the attitudes of longtime churchgoers as the Church's official teaching on homosexuality and, therefore, the final word on what God thinks of them. Feeling they cannot stay Christian with integrity, they head for the hills toward a group of people who will accept them.

While the Church's teachings on sexuality are challenging to members of every sexual orientation, they never, not once, condemn someone's personhood or dignity. They do not ever degrade a person's experience or call them a mistake simply because they happen to struggle with a particular result of the fall. The teachings of the Church claim that every single person, no matter what, is deeply loved by God. God wants every single person in heaven with him, no matter who they are attracted to, but we, the members of the Body of Christ, have sold ourselves as being unwelcoming to sinners.

I remember my mom telling me that about her friend who experienced rejection and judgment from her fellow church parishioners when her son came out of the closet. That is one quick version of the same story over and over again. The message is, "You are welcome unless you are different. Come on in, unless your sin is different or more visible than ours." For fifty years, this message has been sold. It's no wonder our culture is searching for happiness outside of Christ.

I am not writing this chapter to talk about only the Church's stance on homosexuality. Yet this is a hot-button issue and one that is especially close to the hearts of millennials and Generation Z. A growing number of individuals are choosing to identify with a sexuality other than "straight." Still, the culture's perception of how Christianity, Catholicism especially, treats homosexuality and gay marriage reveals a broader issue of how the Church handles the political and societal issues that have become most important to millennials. When it comes to issues such as women's rights, gender identity, freedom of expression, and modern relationships, the Church has in practice earned the reputation of being backward and bigoted.

We have all heard the stories: The Catholic high school student who got pregnant and was forced to leave the school. She was shamed publicly, and her future compromised. She was first met with judgment and condemnation instead of mercy. We know the mother who tried to be faithful to Church teaching but was terrified of getting pregnant for the ninth or tenth time. The black-and-white rules of her Church seemed to keep her under a mountain of diapers and a gaggle of children, and having lost herself entirely in what was supposed to be a vocation to joy.

When it comes to personal choice and freedom of expression, the Catholic Church seems mean to our modern sensibilities. In a world that values tolerance and love over all things, it looks as if being a member of the Church would make you a bigot. Why would anyone want to belong to an organization that has this reputation, both earned and unearned?

It's easy to understand why religious affiliation has declined dramatically over the last twenty years, especially among young people. If you want to be considered nice, then being part of a Church that seems to be at odds with the culture is out of the question.

What I Learned

For years I considered the Church's teaching on contraception to be the most backward of them all. I understood why the Christian religion teaches that we should save sex until marriage, and I was on board with doing just that—forgoing contraception; that was a different ball game. Having a big family would keep me from achieving a high-powered career and building wealth. Such an antiquated rule made no sense, and I had no intention of following it. Why did the Church keep a teaching that was so unpopular in the first place? I had no idea why until I attended a high school chastity talk while I was volunteering for my local youth group in Tampa. At this time, I had committed myself to Catholicism but had not yet fallen in love with this faith.

That night I sat through what I consider to be an okay chastity talk. The speaker was a straight shooter. Her talk had no bells and whistles, no scary threats, just the facts and Catholicism, something I appreciated. After her presentation on chastity, the speaker switched gears from speaking about premarital sex to reflecting on contraception. I had never actually heard someone defend the Church's seemingly indefensible stance formally. I sat up straight and paid attention, unprepared for anything that might challenge my already "well-formed" beliefs.

The speaker articulated the Church's stance beautifully on family planning, but there were two parts to her lecture that just blew me away. In the first part, she spoke about the release of *Humanae Vitae*, the encyclical written by Pope St. Paul VI, which affirmed the Church's stance that artificial contraception is an immoral means of family planning. This papal document, released in 1968, caused a firestorm throughout the Church. Priests, religious, and laypeople alike were patiently waiting for the Church to change its old teaching on family planning to relieve married couples of the burden of large families. When that didn't happen, many Catholics decided to do whatever they wanted anyway.

In the last part of the encyclical, after Pope Paul VI explains God's plan for marriage and family, he affirms a couple's need to space out children and writes that moral family planning is abstaining from intercourse during a woman's fertile period. He then predicts what he believes will happen if artificial contraception becomes widely used. His predictions were that (1) moral standards would lower in broader society, (2) the divorce rate would skyrocket, (3) men would start to view women solely as objects of sexual pleasure, and (4) the government would force birth control on its citizens.[1]

Fifty years after the release of *Humanae Vitae*, it is easy to see that Pope Paul VI's predictions all came true. Considering the prediction on morality, the Victoria's Secret fashion show would have been unthinkable seventy years ago. Today, it is benign compared to even your average music video. Considering the prediction on divorce, in the 1970s the divorce rate rose 70 percent. As far as women being seen as sexual objects, the #MeToo moment rose out of a culture where many men see women as sexual objects meant for their pleasure. And finally, governments such as China with the one-child policy have forced birth control on their citizens to devastating consequences. Even in the United States, religious institutions have had to battle in the courts as the government tries to force them to provide birth control to their employees even if it against these institutions' faith. Fifty years after Pope Paul VI wrote these predictions, the relationships between the sexes is weaker, the family has suffered, and our society is struggling with serious confusion on the meaning and role of sexuality in the human person.

Sitting in the talk, I couldn't ignore just how prophetic the encyclical seemed to be. Could the Church have had a point to make even if its conclusion was so unpopular? I sat there asking myself this question as the speaker started talking about monkeys, the next topic that made my mouth drop.

As she continued with her lecture, she told us about an atheistic social scientist name Lionel Tiger who decided to conduct a bunch of experiments as birth control continued to hit the market in the seventies. He knew that birth control would have a major impact on the social fabric of society and wanted to observe it, so he did what many scientists do: experiments with monkeys.

Tiger confined male and female macaque monkeys to an island and let nature take its course.[2] Within a short amount of time, the alpha males had emerged and chosen female monkeys with whom they would mate. The scientist then started injecting the mated female monkeys with Depo-Provera, a hormonal birth control. The male monkeys stopped mating with those injected females and found other females with whom to mate. The scientists then injected all the females with birth control hormones. The males stopped mating with the females altogether, started acting more aggressively, masturbating, and trying to mate with each other. The scientists stopped injecting the females with birth control hormones, and eventually things went back to normal.

What a crazy story. I sat there, not able to believe my ears. Now I am sure there are a million holes that one could poke through the experiment, but it is clear that messing with the reproductive harmony that exists between males and females has a haywire effect on some level. I had never heard anything like this before, and I didn't even actually believe the speaker. *Catholic lies*, I thought, *I have to find out for myself.*

Sure enough, I went home that night and googled the "Lionel Tiger birth control experiment." It was all there, just as she had explained it. The Catholics hadn't made it up. This man isn't even religious, yet he knew hormonal birth control manipulated the fabric of our relationships.

After learning this, I couldn't unhear the message of the talk. I then worked to learn as much as I reasonably could about the Church's teaching on contraception. I only had to think of my own story and look around me at every aspect of youth culture and pop culture to recognize, plain as day, that something has gone terribly awry between men and women. The Church stood its ground on this teaching because it was right. Yes, it may seem old-fashioned, outdated, or even anti-woman, but the facts reveal that while contraception seems to provide freedom for women, it has actually caused more harm than good. The Church stood on divine wisdom.

The point of me telling this story is not merely to zero in on contraception as a hot-button issue, just as I do not want to focus only on Catholicism's teaching on gay marriage. Yes, the chastity talk I heard catalyzed a slow process in which I started to question why I so vehemently disagreed with some of the Church's teachings and whether I had thought through these things. I hope you decide to challenge yourself in that way too. During this process, I realized something else that I believe is important for millennial Catholics to understand.

The Catholic Church does not make up rules just to be unpopular. These teachings are not born out of the fear of modern culture either. They are not put forth by men and women who get a kick out of seeing the people in the pews bow down in submission. There is nothing sinister, manipulative, or blind about the teachings supported by the Catholic Church. The people who take it upon themselves to "enforce" those teachings may bring with them a whole world of problems. Still, the teachings themselves are based on much deeper history, scripture, and philosophy than most of us have ever applied to our quickly decided social stances. The Church presents to us a life of wisdom. This wisdom flows out of the Gospel given to us by Jesus Christ himself in the scriptures. It has been wrestled with, prayed through, and developed by the holiest, most brilliant minds that have ever existed.

The Church's teachings, especially the hard ones, deserve to, at the very least, be considered with sincerity and humility. Even if we decide that we disagree, which we are free to do, by the way, we should do so after giving the Church a chance to speak. Maybe we aren't as smart as we think. Perhaps the wisdom of the Church is the very thing we need to live a whole, healthy, happy, joyful, and fulfilled life. We owe these teachings the same respect that we would give an older man, full of experience, wounded from years of battle, trying to warn us "young'uns" not to think we are smarter than he when he has lived through so much more than we. Let us at least listen. That night, as I heard that speaker talk about contraception, I learned that I didn't have all the answers. I learned that I needed to listen, and I found myself changing my mind.

Highest Pursuit

Not long after I heard the talk on chastity and contraception, I went to a small art exhibit with a new friend. After we walked through the art exhibit, we sat on a bench outside and started talking about all things Christianity. He is an evangelical who is radically in love with poverty and is one of the most interesting people I have ever met. In turn, I, a Jesus-loving Roman Catholic, seemed like an anomaly to him. As our conversation developed, we discussed most of the "churchy" controversial issues. After covering most of the bases, he asked me what I thought about the Christian stance on homosexual relationships. I fumbled for an orthodox yet socially acceptable answer to give him. I couldn't find one, so I just went with orthodoxy: I told him I believed in the traditional teachings of the Church on marriage and had seen the teachings applied poorly by many believers. I told him I found the teaching to be incredibly difficult because I know so many people who struggle with their sexual identity. I am not always sure it is my place to pontificate to them the teachings of a faith to which they do not subscribe.

He agreed that the subject matter is incredibly difficult, and then he asked me what I believed is the highest thing I could pursue in my life. I hesitated, trying to figure out his angle, and then responded that the highest thing that one can pursue is an intimate relationship with God. He affirmed my answer:

> Yes, a thriving relationship with God is the highest thing anyone can pursue. To know him deeply, to walk with him, and to live every day in knowing God is the ultimate goal of life and will bring us to the ultimate joy. The problem is, most of society believes romance is the ultimate pursuit. We all think that once we find the right romance, we will be the most fulfilled. This thought process, that romance as the highest pursuit of our lives, is demonstrably false, as evidenced by the world around us. Everywhere we look, we see people who have been ravaged by romances gone wrong. Still, we seek romance as our ultimate fulfillment. Most of us do so at the expense of the actual highest good, God. Our lower pursuits, things to which we think we are entitled, get in the way of us pursuing God and responding to his movements in our lives.

He finished, "I think our obsession with sexuality of all sorts is one of the main barriers in our society that keeps us from finding God."

I've never forgotten that conversation. It offered such a paradigm shift for me. We tend to get so hung up on what the "Christian rules" prohibit that we never look to see what they may be promoting. Is it possible that the boundaries and the guardrails exist to help us stay the course as we journey toward our creator? If we strip all the trappings away, are we entitled to any particular lifestyle or choice? And if so, how do we weigh the real trade-offs between our ultimate goals and our immediate lifestyles?

Yes, churchgoers need to do a better job of being the Body of Christ as we try to lead others to that highest pursuit. Those of us in the pews can start by simply listening to others before talking. We can stop leading with the message of behavior modification and instead tell people of Jesus Christ's unending love and the goodness of the Gospel. We can also, through genuine relationship, when appropriate, speak the Truth in love. We can invite others into repentance by sharing our own faults in failures and telling of how God's mercy has transformed us. In the end, it is the Holy Spirit who convicts, and it is the kindness of God that leads us to repentance. If we lead others to God, he in his goodness will do the rest.

The teachings of Christianity in and of themselves are meant to lead us toward the highest good. They point us toward knowing God and living in his order. Because he created us, his law is best for us. The Psalmist writes, "The law of the LORD is perfect, reviving the soul; the testimony of the LORD is sure, making wise the simple; the precepts of the LORD are right, rejoicing the heart; the commandment of the LORD is pure, enlightening the eyes" (Ps 19:7–8). God's law will refresh our souls if we let it.

Why I Stayed

It's been ten years since I sat in that pew and heard the stories of the contracepting monkeys. I know we are in a very small minority, but my husband and I follow all the teachings of the Catholic Church to the very best of our ability—yes, sometimes begrudgingly, but we do try. My husband and I didn't live together or sleep together before we got married. We don't use contraception (our third baby in five years will be here in a month); we tithe on our income, which is far less than it could be if we didn't work in ministry. We follow a lot of rules, rules that probably leave us looking like prudes from the 1950s. I'm not saying this to make us seem especially holy. My life's trajectory and desires had me landing anywhere but here. I would have railed against many of these teachings years ago, and yet here I am, paying, praying, and obeying.

My richer, chicer, more modern imaginary self would be offended by who I have become, and yet in this life—the one in which I have submitted to God—I have found a freedom of which I believe most people dream. Jesus Christ has saved me from damnation, and he has also saved me from a life of futility. So often we think if we can just shed the chains of tradition, we will indeed be free, but we are wrong. Anarchy brings chaos. Seeking only freedom *from* the bad instead of freedom *for* the good will lead us to being controlled by our desires. God wants us to be free from the temptations of this world to find true freedom in him. This is what the Christian life offers us, even if we have to sacrifice other pleasures to get there. The mountain is high and the climb is steep, but the summit is beautiful.

I stayed in the Church because I found truth and wisdom in its teachings that I had never found before. In the folds of Christianity, I have found true freedom. My life isn't perfect, but I am fulfilled. I have broken free of many sins that wreaked havoc over my life. I no longer grasp for this image of the perfect life with all the money, all the friends, and all the stuff, and so I am no longer burdened by being in the hamster wheel of "more." In obedience to God, however, I have held out my hands to receive his blessings and kept them open so he can use me how he pleases.

Regardless of how foolish they look to the world, the teachings of Christianity are not backward; they exist to straighten out crooked hearts, and they will do so if we trust.

Archbishop Fulton Sheen described the Catholic Church in these beautiful terms:

> If I were not a Catholic, and were looking for the true Church in the world today, I would look for the one Church which did not get along well with the world; in other words, I would look for the Church which the world hated. My reason for doing this would be, that if Christ is in any one of the churches of the world today, He must still be hated as He was when He was on earth in the flesh. If you would find Christ today, then find the Church that does not get along with the world. Look for the Church that is hated by the world as Christ was hated by the world. Look for the Church that is accused of being behind the times, as Our Lord was accused of being ignorant and never having learned. Look for the Church which men sneer at as socially inferior, as they sneered at Our Lord because He came from Nazareth. Look for the Church which is accused of having a devil,

as Our Lord was accused of being possessed by Beelze-
bub, the Prince of Devils. Look for the Church which,
in seasons of bigotry, men say must be destroyed in
the name of God as men crucified Christ and thought
they had done a service to God. Look for the Church
which the world rejects because it claims it is infallible,
as Pilate rejected Christ because He called Himself the
Truth. Look for the Church which is rejected by the
world as Our Lord was rejected by men. Look for the
Church which amid the confusion of conflicting opinions, its members love as they love Christ, and respect
its Voice as the very Voice of its Founder, and the suspicion will grow, that if the Church is unpopular with
the spirit of the world, then it is unworldly, and if it is
unworldly, it is other-worldly. Since it is other-worldly,
it is infinitely loved and infinitely hated as was Christ
Himself. But only that which is Divine can be infinitely hated and infinitely loved. Therefore the Church is
Divine.[3]

All of the accusations made of Catholicism and Christianity today
were made of our Lord and Savior two thousand years ago. We may
like to pretend that Jesus was an innocuous hippy, but we should
remember that the crowds wanted him dead for a reason: he challenged the status quo of hypocrisy, complacency, and inequality.

I can only imagine that you have thought the Church to be
dumb and out of touch at one point or another. Maybe it is. But
perhaps it isn't. Have you taken the time to examine the Church
teachings *and* examine your own heart? Maybe the Church has
wisdom from which you could learn. Challenge yourself to sit in
a chapel for fifteen minutes every few days, join a Bible study, or
read from the writings of the saints and the popes. You can google
your questions; just pay attention to your sources. Learn to pray,
and allow yourself to be proven wrong. Don't walk away before you
are sure you are right and the rules are wrong. Catholicism may
just be the thing you need to be set free.

8.

Allowing Jesus to Make Us Happy

What I Experienced

I sat across the table from Joe, unable to believe what I was hearing. I had met him and his family in a Florida airport when I was eighteen. They were fellow Louisianans and had three tiny, blonde children with whom I immediately fell in love and so became their babysitter when I moved to Louisiana State University. Joe and his wife were a joy to be around. They were kind and generous and had enjoyable senses of humor. They seemed to get along as a couple; they were committed Catholics who also happened to be wealthy. Every time I drove away from their house, I asked myself how I could achieve this kind of life myself.

Of course, as providence would have it, my young adult life took me down a trajectory that looked nothing like theirs. At twenty-six, I was fundraising my salary, and I was also on a dating fast, which made "happily married with children on the way" pretty difficult to achieve. I didn't mind. I didn't even think about it. I was on a grand adventure to spread the Gospel, and I rarely thought about the life of which I had once dreamed.

At the end of my first semester as a missionary, I decided to reach out to Joe's wife, Kate. I was going to be in Baton Rouge and wanted to reconnect with them. I remember driving up a mountain with my missionary teammate, Andrea, as I read the word "divorce" in her responding email. *Divorce? What? She and Joe were getting a divorce? How was that even possible?* They seemed to have a perfect life. I had been in their home many times. They had fought once or twice, but who doesn't? I could not believe what I was reading. I was heartbroken for them and their children. I was heartbroken that this marriage had been irreparably broken. After a couple of emails back and forth, I decided that I would visit, even if it was awkward. After all, I wanted to see them. I wanted to hear their story and see their children. I wanted to understand.

A few weeks later, I drove up to the beautiful house where I once helped toddlers ride their bikes. The little toddlers, of course, were no longer toddlers and didn't even really remember me. It was Joe's week at the house, and so I sat across from him at his large, round table as he told me his version of the story. As he spoke to me, I realized I was sitting in front of a totally different man than the one I had known in college. Here before me was a man who had been set free from his "perfect" life.

"My wife and I were both finishing a bottle of wine a night," he told me, and I tried to listen with a neutral face. He continued his story. He did, in fact, have the "perfect life" that I had perceived. Yet I never realized that he and his wife were becoming miserable as they gave themselves over to the bondages of wealth, high society, and social status.

Joe continued, "Finally, I ended up in my local priest's office. I had hit rock bottom. I looked at him and said, 'Father, I can go anywhere, I can do anything, and yet you have the one thing that I want but can't seem to have, and I want to know how to get it.'"

The priest asked Joe what that one thing was. "Peace," he responded. "You have peace. How do I get it?"

The priest, in his simple wisdom, replied, "Joe, you have to surrender; you need to surrender it all to God."

Joe told the priest that surrender was the one thing he didn't do. Luckily for him, surrender was the only option if he wanted to get his life in order. With the guidance of this priest, he did surrender. He ended up getting treatment for his alcohol problem and has been sober ever since. He lost thirty pounds and rededicated himself to God.

As he finished telling me his story, he said to me, "I just took my kids on vacation. I brought three pairs of shorts for the entire time and wasn't bothered a bit. It took a lot for me to realize that none of this stuff matters; what matters is my relationships, and that is my focus."

Whoa. We finished our conversation, and I felt like I needed to catch my breath. I drove away that day so affected by the story I had just heard that I was unable to think of anything else. I wish I could write that Joe and his wife got back together, and all was rainbows and butterflies, but it didn't happen that way. Instead, God does what he always does. He bathed them in mercy. He is the God of our messes, not the ideal that we make up in our minds. He redeems the realities that we create for ourselves in our brokenness.

This is what I realized as I listened to Joe's story. He and his family had to live with the consequences of his choices. They had built a lifestyle they couldn't sustain, and so something had to break; in this case, it was their marriage. Through humility and surrender, however, Joe renewed his relationship with God.

I drove away that day permanently changed by our conversation. I was still sad about all that had happened, but it seemed as if Joe had become a man of hope and joy, a gift that can only come from the living God, not any of the perfection after which we chase.

I kept coming back to one question as I pondered our conversation. *Why does it take a catastrophe for us to turn to God?* Or to put it another way: *Why don't we believe God will make us happy?* Joe, after trying to get his wife to leave the Catholic Church, ended up becoming Catholic himself. He told me he was appalled to find out that Catholicism is true. From before they ever got engaged, he knew the Catholic Church was true. He knew the Gospel. Why didn't he own it? Why didn't he recognize the Gospel promise that true worship of the living God brings all happiness? The scriptures say, "But seek first his kingdom and his righteousness, and all these things shall be yours as well" (Mt 6:33). He knew this, and yet there was something in him that doubted that God alone was enough. He spent years chasing idols only to crash, burn, and come back to what he had known in the very beginning. I can relate because I had done the same. Most of us end up turning to God as a last resort.

I spent years of my life chasing the wind when the Lord was holding his hand out to me, offering the peace for which I longed. It is the very rare individual who knows that God alone is sufficient and just runs with that from the very beginning. Most of us make Christianity a nice hobby at best because, at the heart of the matter, we just don't believe God will satisfy. We acknowledge the Lord with our lips, but our hearts are far from him. We wave off the crucifix as we run toward everything else because we just don't believe Jesus is the answer.

Many times I have tried to convince my toddlers that vegetables are better for them than candy. They trust me to a certain extent, and so they can repeat my words that plants make you strong and candy is a treat—but in the end, candy just tastes better. Never mind that if you only eat candy ever, you will get sick. The stuff that actually is good for our bodies just doesn't initially taste as good as the fake stuff. Sin is the same way. It is crafted to feel better than virtue initially. Creation is beautiful, but without being enjoyed properly, within the order of the Creator, it will destroy us. We chase after it anyway, just as my toddlers are always trying to sneak candy.

The Lord has promised us that he would give us life in abundance (see John 10:10). To our naked eyes, though, it just doesn't really seem as if that's true. With the allure of all the other "happiness" that we are offered, most of us choose to eat, drink, and be merry unless a problem arises. We leave the Church because we don't, in the end, believe that God can fulfill our desires. If he can't, but something else can, then why should we stay?

What I Learned

You know the kind of day in which nothing is wrong, but nothing is right? It had been three months since I'd become a youth minister, and I was just sitting in my office, agitated, getting nothing done. There was a restlessness within me that I needed to ease, and so I decided to turn to one of my go-to comforts.

One consideration was to treat myself to some M&Ms from the office next door, but I knew that five would turn into fifty. I thought about getting a latte, but I always got a latte. I then remembered the Marshalls down the street. Few things feel as good as finding a bargain, so I settled on a quick shopping trip. Finishing my next task, I hopped in my car and drove to the outdoor mall. Walking into the store, I was ready for calm to soothe my restless heart.

That calm never came.

My restlessness grew as I looked around the store. I knew I could pick up a pair of shoes, a cute top, or something for my apartment, but whatever the purchase, it would lose its luster within a half hour.

My favorite pastor once called new things "the stuff of future garage sales." His words echoed in my mind as I sadly made my way for the exit empty-handed.

Four years before I had given my life to Jesus Christ. After years of trying to stop chasing what would not make me happy, I should have been pleased with my felt recognition of the futility of material possessions, but I didn't. Instead, I felt a loss. For most of my life, I, like the rest of society, had been a well-trained American consumer.

Fashion made me happy. Wearing pretty things made me feel validated, and I fully expected to continue this habit for the rest of my life, hopefully making enough money to buy fancier, more couture things. My Marshalls experience was a needed but unwelcome wake-up call. The counterfeit version of happiness was familiar. What would happen if I stopped going for the false pleasures first and Jesus second? What if I let go of everything else and always pursued a relationship with Jesus before anything else?

I knew I didn't need more stuff. I needed something that would last, something that wouldn't fade right after I bought it or come with a delayed dose of buyer's remorse. I needed communion with the living God. Do you know how unglamorous this realization is? I simply needed to be with God.

Soberly and a little let down, I drove back to the chapel at my parish and sat in silence until peace flooded my soul. There was nothing flashy about the old Catholic chapel, but God's presence was exactly what I needed. Our God is not always the God we want, but he is always the God we need. I knew I would no longer be filled by the stuff of future garage sales or anything else that came with it. It had become clear to me in my life and the lives that I saw around me that these things were pleasures and pleasures were flighty little things that left emptiness in their wake. We weren't made for comfort; we were made for lasting joy, a joy that only God can give.

All of us know on some level that the trinkets we pursue are only temporary pleasures, and yet we seek them anyway. Why did I want so badly for some stupid shirt at Marshalls to fill my emptiness that day? Why did Joe still chase the world after he converted to Catholicism even though he recognized that Catholicism was the Truth? Neither of us, at the end of the day, actually believed that the God of our religion would actually make us most happy.

King Solomon, the son of King David, is considered to be one of the wisest men who ever lived. In the first book of Kings, the Lord appeared to Solomon and said, "Ask what I shall give you" (3:5). Solomon answered, "Give thy servant therefore an understanding mind to govern thy people, that I may discern between good and evil" (3:9). The Lord, pleased with Solomon's response, replies, "I now do according to your word. Behold, I give you a wise and discerning mind, so that none like you has been before you and none like you shall arise after you" (3:12). At the beginning of Ecclesiastes, King Solomon proclaims a truth we all know, yet don't want to acknowledge: "Vanity of vanities, says the Preacher, vanity of vanities! All is vanity. . . . The eye is not satisfied with seeing, nor the ear filled with hearing. What has been is what will be, and what has been done is what will be done; and there is nothing new under the sun" (1:2, 8–9).

Our eyes are never satisfied by shiny new objects; our ears are never filled with praises from the world. History shows us this time and time again, yet we continue our misguided pursuits. This is at the heart of our original sin: we chase after what is meaningless. We fool ourselves into thinking that the next thing will make us happy, and so we become constant consumers, never pausing to ask ourselves if it is all worth it until we hit a wall and are forced to reevaluate. Only when all else fails do we finally pay attention to what we know and begin to give God a chance to do what only he can do: lead us onto a path of life.

Even though this attitude is countercultural, if we look we can find examples of men and women who "had it all" and gave it up for a life with God.

A few years ago, I watched a short HBO documentary[1] on the life of Dolores Hart, a major movie star in the fifties and sixties. She made ten films in five years and acted alongside major Hollywood stars such as Elvis Presley. She was a young beauty and, again, had everything that the world could possibly offer her. Yet in the middle of her budding career, Hart abruptly announced that she would be joining a convent to become a Benedictine nun.

As she told her story fifty years later, the wonder still shone in her eyes. After she had performed on Broadway for nine months, her friend suggested that she visit the Abbey of Regina Laudis in Connecticut to get some rest. At first she said no. She had no desire to be around nuns, but her friend insisted and eventually persuaded Dolores to go. There, in the quiet of the abbey, Dolores found peace. She found herself and fell in love with God. She returned to Hollywood after her time in the abbey, but she would never be able to fully embrace the life she was living. There was always the faint calling of religious life. As her career continued to grow, she met and fell in love with Don Robinson. They got engaged and everything was set for them to be married in a big, beautiful wedding. After an engagement party, however, Don asked her why she seemed so distant. It was then that she told him that she was answering the call to religious life. She broke off her engagement and entered the Abbey of Regina Laudis in her wedding dress in 1963. She had fallen in love with God, and she knew that nothing

short of him, not even the fame and fortune of which so many
dream, would ever satisfy her.

In the comment section of the documentary on YouTube, people berated Hart as a woman who has thrown her life away. Any
glance at her picture, however, reveals a woman who has a peace
that most of the world will never know.

At one point in the documentary, another sister shares why
she entered the convent. She says she started to visit the abbey at
a time when feminism was a significant part of the American cultural current. She commented, "Many of us saw Mother Dolores,
Mother Abbess. We sensed in them liberated women who had
found a love in their lives that we were searching for." This is the
effect that God has on our souls when we trust him. He liberates.
He straightens our crooked hearts and transforms our intelligence
into wisdom. This concept needs little support. We simply need to
assess our culture and decide if we become better or more joyful
when we buy into its marketing. Or is it possible that the God of
old is being honest when he says that he made our hearts for him.
What could he do in our lives if we would only believe him when
he speaks to our hearts? If we realized that we will be restless until
we decide to let God be the one to make us happy?

When we as a generation come to understand this concept, we
will be able to live with true wisdom. Most of us are pretty smart,
but few of us are truly wise. We have enough pleasure in which we
can drown ourselves, but few of us have lasting joy. For lasting joy
comes only from God and the integrity of living for him. It is the
only thing that will bring peace to our souls.

Why I Stayed

Again, I sat in the chapel; this time, my failures were screaming at
me. There are some days when I sit down to pray as if I am a little
angel, light as a feather, and ready to fly to the heavens to meet my
God. This was not that day. Whether it was my gossiping, my pride,
my judgmental heart, or all of them, I don't remember, but the
feeling of unworthiness overwhelmed me. Why was I even there?

I tried to ignore the feeling as I opened my Bible, but I eventually had to sit with myself, my guilt, and my shame.

I then realized how much I doubted the Gospel message: I didn't truly accept that God loved me, despite my sin, and wanted to redeem me. It hit me that on my worst days, and my best days, I can sit and talk to God because of what *he* did. If I only depend on myself to be in God's good graces, I will never be there. St. Paul tells us that there is no condemnation in Christ Jesus. He also tells us that we are saved by faith through grace; this is a gift from God so that no one may boast. On my best day—when I was the most pious, the most generous, and the most "holy"—I had nothing to boast about because God did the saving. I accepted that salvation, and yes, there is a response of faith in which I can now step into the good works he has prepared for me, but in no way can I take credit for my goodness. It is all grace. In the same vein, I should not wallow in my faults, failures, and sins, for there is nothing that cannot be covered by the Cross of Christ.

I am a Catholic because it is in the folds of the Catholic Church that I can find real joy. Jesus Christ, through his Church, offers us lasting fulfillment. Of course, we in the Church, in our failings, have done very little to market that joy to the world, but nevertheless it waits for us.

In the Catholic Church I can come to terms with myself, shed my shame, and accept redemption. This alone is more valuable than anything else. Non-Catholics frequently joke about "Catholic guilt," but I think this is the pot calling the kettle black. When our choices are informed by faith, we're freed; when our choices are dictated by sin, we're racked with shame. How many of us are still carrying the burdens of choices we made in college? How many of us are hiding within our hearts the constant weight of old sins? Is it possible that the shame of our failures keeps us chasing the wind because we are hiding from the living God, just as Adam and Eve did in the garden of Eden? Every day we are offered an illusion, and seeking it leaves us with genuine consequences.

The Church offers us a solution. Within the silence of its walls, we can come to terms with exactly who we are. It is hard to ignore what is pressing on our hearts when there are no distractions. The

Church reveals the truth that if God can redeem one person, he can redeem us all.

Now, as a Catholic, I have found the forgiveness that I need to allow peace to reign in my soul. The pressure was never on me; it was on him, and he delivered. My role is to accept the gift and share the gift. That's it. When I am trying to impress the world, I take on a whole host of burdens. All of a sudden, I have to be the perfect mother and wife, a combination of Betty Crocker, Joanna Gaines, a CEO, and a super fun and free thirtysomething. The weight of this is crushing. Within the Church, I only have to be God's, and everything else flows from that.

I can't stress enough that this doesn't mean my life is perfect or that you can find me floating around my house with wings and a halo. I still struggle with my sin. I still gossip, give in to pride and envy—sometimes in very selfish and immature ways. I see successful women on Instagram and secretly wish they weren't so successful. I compare my house, kids, and husband to others. I gossip way more than I should (the worst!).

The difference now, though, is that even on my worst day I am compelled to run to the Lord in my home, in the chapel, or in the confessional and know that I am forgiven. He has taken the burden and removed the shame. He also guides me along a path toward sanctity, and when I look back over the years, I see progress. I can see times when I chose to forgo the gossip and just decide that everyone is doing the best they can. I can see that I chose gratitude for all that God has given to me, reveled in my own life, over comparing my life to someone else's. I can see the times when I was able to give mercy and let go of the grudge. I recognize I want God more today than I did yesterday, and I am filled with hope for the future that God will complete the work he started in me.

When I decided I would give God the chance to make me happy, I had no idea how far he would go to do so. I often find myself in awe of his salvation. Not only has he saved my soul from eternal damnation (no big deal), but also he saved my earthly life from futility. I look at my life and the joy that I have found. I did not do it. I did not earn it. I don't deserve it.

Left to my own devices, I would be living a polished disaster. I would have ended up on the wrong career path because I was too afraid to leave the facade of success behind or would have gotten married for the wrong reasons. I definitely would not have the children I have. And I would probably be in debt from trying to keep up with the Joneses. Surrounded by a life I could control, everyone would have been impressed, but a quiet emptiness would have kept me up at night as I wondered if there was more to life.

Yet by following the life that Jesus asks us to live in his Church, I have found fulfillment, meaning, beauty, relationships, and joy. I think this happens in part because God makes simple what we make complicated. The Jewish people have 613 commandments in the Old Testament.[2] Jesus boiled it down to two: love God with all of your being, and love your neighbor as yourself. The more I follow the Lord, the more he clears the path of all that distracts me (the modern idols that distract us all) and focuses me on those three things: loving him, loving others, and loving the good.

First, the more I spend time in prayer and in the scriptures, the more I fall in love with the Lord. He is good. He is the point of everything. That's it. All roads should lead to God, and if they don't, they are not worth going down. The bigger he has become in my life, the smaller everything else has become, enabling me to choose him more often.

Second, the more I strive to love others, the more I find joy in living out the call to serve my family. I am a wife and a mother to three beautiful daughters. These are my people. I am not just called but also commanded to give my life to them and to help get them to heaven. If I were to put something else before them, I would have conflict within my heart because I would know I am called to put them first. Now this doesn't mean I don't pursue anything else; I have a job, and I am writing this book. What it does mean is they are always my first priority. In all honesty, I have battled my loss of personal autonomy greatly since I became a wife and a mother, and yet as I look as this little family that my husband and I have created, I find myself content and at the same time overcome with joy. I could not be more grateful. I would not have chosen this exact life, but God knew better than me.

Finally, the more I fall in love with God, the more I fall in love with the "good" things in life, such as the pursuit of wisdom and knowledge. Jesus renews our spirit, so I just don't like some of the things I used to like. Music by Lil Wayne and episodes of *Dexter* just don't do it for me anymore. I have become vigilant about the books I read, the TV shows I watch, and the podcasts I listen to. This doesn't mean I only watch sappy, G-rated films. I said I fell in love with not the saccharine but the good. There is a difference, and I ensure that the media I consume lifts my spirit and leads me into some form of truth, beauty, or goodness.

All of these things have led me to value people over things, virtue over vice, and God over everything else. God isn't a genie. He isn't here to give me health, wealth, and comfort. He never promises a life without pain or suffering, but he does promise joy. I am living proof of that joy.

Friend, there is a good chance that you or a loved one have walked away from Jesus and Catholicism because it doesn't seem to make people happy. I get that. On many levels, it doesn't seem to make people happy because we make God look more like a task-master than a lover. I invite you to take another look. What are you chasing in your life? Is it the wind? Do you keep going from one thing to the next because the first thing no longer satisfies? Are you unable to quiet the distractions for fear of what a moment of silence might bring? The Lord offers you the only thing under the sun that can bring true joy to your soul: himself. He wants to lead you into a life filled with meaning. He could be inviting you into something that looks as different from your present experience as the difference between the life of a Hollywood actress and a Roman Catholic nun. If his promise is true, isn't it worth it? Sit in a chapel for fifteen minutes, and let the Lord speak to your heart. Don't miss out on the chance to respond to his love.

9.

Embracing The Heroism of "Gloomy" Saints

What I Experienced

C. S. Lewis said, "We are half-hearted creatures, fooling about with drink and sex and ambition when infinite joy is offered us, like an ignorant child who wants to go on making mud pies in a slum because he cannot imagine what is meant by the offer of a holiday at the sea. We are far too easily pleased."[1] With this quote he gets it exactly right. Every one of us is guilty of this. We place far too high a premium on our mediocre notion of happiness when our God calls us to lives of fearless heroism.

During my second year serving as a missionary, I received a call from a friend who was in crisis mode. What was his crisis? He met a woman he really liked. He started to tell me all of these wonderful things about her. She was funny, cute, interesting, and somewhat unassuming. She seemed to have everything he was looking for in a girlfriend, but he finished by telling me that he couldn't date her. "Why? What's the problem?" I asked. "She won't sleep with me," he responded. I always appreciated it when my friends were bluntly honest with me about their non-Catholic actions, despite my Catholic missionary status.

As we continued the discussion, he told me she was pretty firmly committed to saving herself for marriage, but he was not interested in waiting until marriage to have sex again and was unwilling to get married anytime soon. It was apparent that he liked her, but her stance was a deal-breaker for him. I challenged him. I asked him what his initial solution to the situation should be, and he told me he would typically wait a few months and try to get her to sleep with him anyway. Again, I appreciated the honesty, and I tried to react neutrally. But then he said, "Mallory, I'm just not that good of a guy." Ouch.

That is not what I saw in my friend. I saw a great man who was shying away from the potential for greatness because, like all of us, he grew up in a culture that messaged anything but self-sacrifice or delayed gratification. From movies and music to friends who are also getting their notions on happiness from American marketing, he received the message that we all did: indulging in our pleasure will bring us maximum freedom and happiness. So, when he wanted to have sex before marriage, he didn't see a reason to rethink this impulse or wait for a woman who didn't.

I took my friend out of his big picture reflections on his character and asked him if he thought he could honor this woman's stance for three months. I told him he had slept with other women that he did not marry, so what if he tried something new and accepted her wishes for three months and then reassessed their relationship at the end? Three months is not a lifetime, and he would have a good idea of how he felt about her by then. If he was falling for her, he should continue to date her, and if not, he could move on and find a woman with lower standards. He liked the idea and said he could probably give it a shot. We got off the phone. They continued their relationship. I don't know the details of how the rest of their dating relationship unfolded. What I do know is that they are now married, and he is deeply in love with her.

One of the tragedies of our human condition is that most of us know we are meant to be great, but we don't believe we can be. My friend told me point-blank that he was "not that good of a guy." This is a lie from hell, and too often it is the message we secretly tell ourselves in the darkness of our hearts. We foster it as we repeatedly excuse ourselves from rising to the occasion. We convince ourselves that certain standards of morality are unreasonable in the first place. We tell ourselves lies such as "I know I should forgive them, but God can't expect me to forgive something so egregious!"; and "If I help that homeless person, I'm supporting their addiction. There are homeless shelters for a reason; I'll become generous when I'm making more money." We then settle for living our lives falling short of who we could be and knowing somewhere in the recesses of our soul that we could be better—we just don't want to be.

I've seen this unfolding in my own life many times. Looking back on my college career I think of how I missed an opportunity to grow in knowledge every time I waited till the last minute to study. I think of where I would be today if I had used my free time to pursue excellence instead of bingeing on shows illegally (this was before the Netflix binge was invented). Looking at my life now, there are countless times that I have heard the voice of the Lord telling me to have a conversation, stop to help someone, give a little more money, or slow down to be present to my children. Often, I convince myself that it is not God telling me this and I go about attending to my present distractions. When I do this, I am saying no to becoming the kind of woman that God knows our world needs at this time.

One of my biggest struggles with the Catholic Church is that its teachings challenge me to be better than I want to be, to give more than I want to give, and to have more integrity than I want to have. I've had to tell myself no again and again when I just want to do what I want to do. I don't want to practice the self-discipline or rise to the virtue of holiness or heroism. It seems to be too much when I can easily settle for mediocrity and have society applaud me for it. Every time I choose to settle, however, I am left wondering what it would be like if I responded to these challenges instead of shying away from them. Who could I be? Who am I supposed to be, and is it possible for me to get there?

What I Learned

I used to hate when people would start talking about the lives of the saints. My eyes would glaze over when I heard a priest say "We are called to be saints." If I wanted an exciting life, it seemed as if becoming a saint was the last thing I needed to do. Seriously, is there anything more boring to look at than a saint statue or a saint card? The halos and the overly pious positions of each little human cherub was enough to send me running for the nearest rave.

For years, I found the statues of the Virgin Mary the least attractive of all. When I looked at her, I just didn't relate to the folded hands, the eyes to heaven, and the porcelain complexion that radiates perfect humility and obedience. My dream job is Broadway; I am anything but quiet, pious, or submissive. If a saint statue accurately depicts the life for which we should be striving, it's no wonder most of us aren't interested. The Catholic Church has a serious marketing problem when it comes to sainthood. We take our crown jewels of holiness and make them look as dull as possible—when the stories of the saints and their actual lives are some of the craziest, most uplifting, and challenging stories I have ever read.

As I returned to my Catholic faith, I learned about the lives of the incredible saints of the Church. All of them had different struggles and different victories, and took different paths to fall in love with the Lord. They are real-life heroes, the very best that our world has to offer, and the more I read about them, the more I am inspired to be like them.

While there are thousands of saints to learn about, I find the modern ones the most interesting because they lived, worked, and worshipped in times similar or much worse than ours. One of my favorite saints is St. Teresa of Calcutta. As a little girl who wanted to be just like Britney Spears, I found her uninteresting. When I looked at her, I perceived that her life was boring, mostly spent in a chapel being overly pious. I couldn't have been more wrong. Little Anjezë, who would grow up to become Mother Teresa, was always faithful.[2] She never strayed far from God, and because of this (not despite it), her life has all the makings of a great adventure story. It was daring, filled with devotion, miracles, and hardship. She indeed was a hero in our time.

One of my favorite stories about Mother Teresa includes the time that she crossed through war-torn Beirut to save thirty-seven orphans. Israel had encircled West Beirut in what they called "Operation Peace for Galilee," and Mother Teresa found out through the French news that orphans with mental illness had been abandoned in Beirut amid the fighting. There was no one to care for them, and so the little children had been left to their own devices. Mother Teresa showed up on the scene, asking to be driven across Beirut to retrieve the orphans and bring them to the nearest local Missionaries of Charity home.

The priest to whom she was talking told her that the risk was too high. "A priest had been killed in the fighting in the two weeks prior," he shared.

Mother Teresa responded, "We must go and take the children one by one. Risking our lives is in the order of things. All for Jesus. All for Jesus. You see, I've always seen things in this light. A long time ago, when I picked up the first person (from a street in Calcutta), if I had not done it that first time, I would not have picked up 42,000 after that. One at a time, I think."[3]

I'd like to note that this happened in 1982. Mother Teresa died in 1997. Can you imagine just how many people she helped in her lifetime if by 1982 she had already personally helped 42,000 people? Insane.

As the conversation continued, Mother Teresa revealed that she had asked Our Lady for a ceasefire to occur the next day since it was one of Our Lady's feast days. Philip Habib, the American ambassador who was part of the conversation, told Mother Teresa that she should have given Our Lady more time. But, he said, if there *were* a ceasefire the next day, he would personally make arrangements for her to go get the orphans.

I know you can guess the ending. Ambassador Habib was able to negotiate a ceasefire the next day, and the four-foot-eleven nun from Albania made her way across the city in total silence. One at a time, she retrieved the abandoned children to be taken out of harm's way and into the care of the Sisters of Charity. Witnesses noted that there were children in the orphanage who had no mental illness but had started to mimic the other children in their abandonment. Once they were in Mother Teresa's arms, they changed.

The story itself is enough to bring one to tears. I am choking back my own emotions as I type this. Yet it isn't just an inspiring story for us to read about and applaud. It's a challenge for us. Mother Teresa was born into original sin, just like you and me. She could have considered God's call on her life and decided it was too hard or unnecessary. Anjezë could have been an average Catholic in Albania living out most of her life, not ruffling any feathers or suffering to spread the Gospel. She could have counted on some other holy person to do the work that she ended up doing and shied away from the heroism to which God called her. She could have still gone to heaven, but no history book would know her name. There would have been no Mother Teresa, just a nice young Catholic who didn't rock the boat.

Thank God she didn't do that. Instead, she leaned into her redemption, and she did "all for Jesus." When you truly love, there are no limits. There is no limit to how far the Father went for us. Our response, even in our brokenness, should be the same. People become saints when they decide there is no limit to their love for God. They go all in, and the whole world becomes better for it.

Every time I learn something about Mother Teresa's life, I am even more blown away. I once tried to find a good quote of hers about mission for a talk, and I could not find one. She dedicated her whole life to her mission, but all I could find were quotes about Jesus Christ. Every single thing she did in her life was for Jesus. It was her love for him that drove her to become a sister, first in the Sisters of Loreto and then in her obstacle-ridden road to founding the Missionaries of Charity. Mother Teresa's love for Christ drove her to pick up possibly hundreds of thousands of people off the street, seeing Christ's face in each of them.

Mother Teresa's life was anything but boring. Her passion for God gave her unrelenting boldness and unrelenting faith. This little woman, who spent much of her life as a humble teacher, worked closely with the who's who of the world stage, such as Princess Diana, and spoke blunt truths on the value of life to power players such as Hillary Clinton. This is the glory that God portrays in a life given to him with no excuses. It is this power that I shy away from when I tell myself "I don't need to be that holy" or "I am not that good of a woman." God made me to be that holy. He asks me to let him make me that good of a woman.

And St. Teresa of Calcutta is one in a crowd of saints whose lives are remarkable. Recently, a good friend was asking me what Catholics believe about forgiveness. I shared that Catholics believe in forgiveness at all costs. I told her the process is messy but that in the end, if we don't forgive, we are the ones who are in bondage. As a devout Anglican, she agreed with me, but she shared that in a recent experience, the Catholics she encountered hadn't embraced this teaching: She had posted something on social media about forgiveness in regard to a terrible act of evil and tragedy that occurred in her community—and all the Catholics jumped down her throat. They claimed we don't have to forgive if the person isn't sorry. They said she was insensitive to suggest such a thing, and an internet mob ensued. The call to heroic virtue was too high a price for these Catholics.

What would it be like if we embraced the example of Jesus and countless saints, and offered a kind of reckless forgiveness? I apologized to my friend for the experience she'd had with Catholic forgiveness and shared the story of St. Josephine Bakhita. Josephine was enslaved in the 1800s in what is now Sudan; she was brutally tortured by her captors. She was taken to Italy and converted to Catholicism, and the Italian courts declared her free because slavery had been outlawed there. She became a religious sister renowned for her kind and happy demeanor with students and visitors to the community. One of her students asked her, "What would you do if you were to meet your captors?" Without hesitation, she responded, "If I were to meet those who kidnapped me, and even those who tortured me, I would kneel and kiss their hands. For, if these things had not happened, I would not have been a Christian and a religious today."[4] If all Catholics emulated St. Josephine's forgiveness, think what an amazing witness we could be to the world!

Another remarkable saint, St. Maximillian Kolbe, volunteered to die in the place of a father while he was a prisoner in Auschwitz.

For most of my life, I only knew this one fact about him. What I didn't realize is that he was a major evangelist in Europe before World War II, and he was fiercely devoted to the Blessed Mother and a faithful son of the Church. He used the latest technology of his time to reach thousands of people in Poland with the message of the Gospel through the ministry he founded called the "Militia Immaculata." His repeated yes to God built him into the kind of man who could commit the ultimate act of love and lay down his life for the sake of another.

While the fruits of his work are still around, his legacy was solidified in his death, his act of love. His immediate life's work was destroyed by circumstances out of his control, and yet his love lasted. It is the same for us: our life's work, no matter how important it is, can be destroyed in an instant, and all that will matter is how we loved or didn't love.

As I learn about the lives of the saints, I hope I can become like them. When we decide that we will allow ourselves to become who we were made to be, even if that is scary, we give the Lord freedom to move as he wishes in us and through us. The life of a saint is the most worthy life there is, regardless of what a dull statue may suggest.

And speaking of statues, back to the Blessed Mother. Over the years, I have fallen in love with Our Lady as I have come to understand her better. Years ago, I heard a sister address the issue of Mary's statues looking overly pious. She said that while Mary can look too meek and obedient to the modern woman, we can forget what it is that she is actually doing in many of her statues. She, our mother, with barely a smirk on her face, is crushing the head of Satan himself, and she isn't even breaking a sweat. *Mic drop.* Mary, in her obedience to God, defeats evil and makes it look easy. This is the kind of strength God is calling us to. He is calling us to be the best the Church has to offer, to offer our best to this world as his ambassadors. It is a high call but one that is reachable if we would only drop our excuses and let God work in us.

Why I Stayed

Walking into St. Peter's Square in the Vatican is a delight. The first time I entered it, I was greeted by the colossal presence of St. Peter's Basilica to the left. Pictures just don't do it justice. Across the square I saw the papal apartments and the balcony where popes greet the world upon their election to the papacy. And then of course I saw the people. There were thousands of people in the square waiting for Pope Francis to give his Wednesday address. Most breathtaking to me were the ninety white saint statues that towered over and around me in the courtyard of the square. They are impossible to miss, and for me, they represent a message that is impossible to shake. Catholicism has been a sign of contradiction in countless ways over the course of history. The saints know something we don't, as they, members of the Church Victorious, stand more closely to heaven than we, the Church Militant, still battling our way on earth. These saints remind us that we should never be distracted by the clamor of this world and that we must keep our hearts oriented toward God. They ran the race and won the ultimate prize, God himself.

As I gazed up that these faith giants, the words of Hebrews 11 and 12 rang out in my heart and soul. St. Paul is telling the story of the faithful from Abraham to his present day. In chapter 11, he breaks into a litany of faith:

> And what more shall I say? For time would fail me to tell of Gideon, Barak, Samson, Jephthah, of David and Samuel and the prophets—who through faith conquered kingdoms, enforced justice, received promises, stopped the mouths of lions, quenched raging fire, escaped the edge of the sword, won strength out of weakness, became mighty in war, put foreign armies to flight. Women received their dead by resurrection. Some were tortured, refusing to accept release, that they might rise again to a better life. Others suffered mocking and scourging, and even chains and imprisonment. They were stoned, they were sawn in two, they were killed with the sword; they went about in skins of sheep

and goats, destitute, afflicted, ill-treated—of whom the
world was not worthy. . . . Therefore, since we are surrounded by so great a cloud of witnesses, let us also lay
aside every weight, and sin which clings so closely, and
let us run with perseverance the race that is set before
us. (Heb 11:32–38, 12:1)

When I read of the lives of those who have gone before me who
gave their lives to Jesus, I get chills. God wrote crazy adventures of
conversion, miracles, sacrifices, and victories with their lives. He
used them for his glory and purpose, the salvation and sanctifica-
tion of the world. Is there a better life to live? Is there a worthier
cause than to participate in bringing mankind back to God? The
witnesses who have gone before us are a testament to the power of
God and fostering our faith through the Church.

There is not a week that goes by in my life in which I am not
frustrated with the institutional Church and the ways it has messed
up so many wonderful things over the years. There is no doubt
that the sins of the Church are many, and they run deep. The obvi-
ous problems of the Church desperately need to be addressed and
fixed. It should first be a welcoming avenue for all to enter into a
loving relationship with God, a life of repentance, joy, and service
to others. There are bad parishes. There are corrupt members of
the clergy and bad teachers. There are examples of bad Catholics
everywhere, and there is no doubt that we all have our scars from
this institution, just as we have scars from every other relationship
and institution in existence. Sin hurts people; that's its point.

There are many reasons to walk away from Jesus and his
Church, but there is something that will never change. When I
walk into any given Catholic church, anywhere in the world, Jesus
Christ himself can be found in the flesh: quiet, humble, perfect,
and loving. He is there waiting for a broken world to come to him
for rest and redemption. At any Catholic church in the world, I can
walk in a sinner and walk out bathed in the mercy of our Lord. At
any Mass ever said, I can receive the Body, Blood, Soul, and Divinity
of Jesus Christ, who gives me rest from my life's storms.

Here, as a Catholic, I am surrounded by a great cloud of witnesses who have already run the race and are now in heaven. They challenge me to throw off everything that hinders me and the sin that so easily entangles. If Jesus Christ is the Lord of the universe and he left for us a Church, that Church is going to have problems until he comes back, and yet he still challenges us to be faithful.

Regardless of its institutional failures, the life to which Catholicism invites us is a life of joy and fulfillment. It is a life that the world cannot and never has been able to offer. It's a chance to get off the gerbil wheel, sit in his presence, and be quenched by his truth and love.

There are so many valid criticisms of Catholicism that those in the Church need to hear and heed. I get them, I understand them, and I am so sorry they exist because they are a significant barrier for so many to the life for which they were meant. Humbly, I ask you to consider if it just might be worth going after Jesus Christ and a life of faith anyway. I ask you to consider if the life you are living now is freer and more fulfilled than one spent in communion with the God of the universe. The Church offers a framework for living out the Gospel personally and communally. That is all it has to be.

I hope that no matter where you are, no matter how you have been hurt or frustrated or disaffected, you will be knocked off your feet by the realization of how much God loves you. He doesn't just love you; he finds you delightful. He longs for you, and he wants your freedom. I hope you realize and respond by falling in love with your God. I hope you return to the Lord with repentance, love, and faithfulness. And then, I hope you find his Truth, waiting to set you free in his broken and beautiful Church.

1. Going beyond Mediocre Masses

1. Center for Applied Research in the Apostolate, "Frequently Requested Church Statistics," https://cara.georgetown.edu/frequently-requested-church-statistics/.

2. Luther's Collected Works, Wittenberg Edition, no. 7 p, 391; as quoted in "Martin Luther on the Real Presence," Bread From Heaven, https://bfhu.wordpress.com/2011/05/13/martin-luther-on-the-real-presence/.

3. Ignatius of Antioch, "Letter to the Romans [A.D. 110]," in "Ignatius of Antioch on the Eucharist," St. Paul Center, December 6, 2010, https://stpaulcenter.com/ignatius-of-antioch-on-the-eucharist.

4. Justin Martyr, *First Apology*, as quoted in the *Catechism of the Catholic Church* 1345.

5. R.R. Reno, "The Francis Effect," *First Things* (podcast), August 26, 2016, https://www.firstthings.com/media/the-francis-effect.

6. Anne Marie Schmidt, *To Hell and Back: Divine Love and the Cross*, Lighthouse Talks (Sycamore, IL: Lighthouse Catholic Media, 2009).

2. Choosing More than Blissful Ignorance

1. C. S. Lewis, *The Screwtape Letters* (New York: HarperCollins, 1996), 59.

2. Fulton Sheen, *Treasure in Clay* (Newark, NJ: Audible, 2018).

3. R. R. Reno, "Return of the Strong Gods," *First Things*, May 2017, https://www.firstthings.com/article/2017/05/return-of-the-strong-gods.

4. David Wong, "7 Reasons the 21st Century Is Making You Miserable," Cracked, September 9, 2007, https://www.cracked.com/article_15231_7-reasons-21st-century-making-you-miserable.html.

5. Lewis, *Screwtape Letters*, 65.

3. Finding Real Answers to Good Questions

1. Taylor Marshall, "Michael Voris Tells His Story (Dr. Taylor Marshall #194)," YouTube, December 20, 2018, https://youtube.com.

2. David Masci and Greg Smith, "7 Facts about American Catholics," Pew Research, October 18, 2018, https://www.pewresearch.org/fact-tank/2018/10/10/7-facts-about-american-catholics/.

3. Mark M. Gray, "Lapsed Catholics Weigh In on Why They Left the Church," OSV, October 22, 2014, https://osvnews.com/2014/10/22/lapsed-catholics-weigh-in-on-why-they-left-church/.

4. Christian Smith, *Young Catholic America* (New York: Oxford University Press, 2014), 10.

5. Smith, *Young Catholic America*, 10.

6. William D'Antonio, James Davidson, Dean Hoge, and Katherine Myer, *American Catholics: Gender, Generation, and Commitment* (Walnut Creek, CA: AltaMira Press, 2001), 4.

7. Smith, *Young Catholic America*, 12–19.

8. "Transcript: JFK's Speech on His Religion," NPR, December 5, 2007, https://www.npr.org/templates/story/story.php?storyId=16920600.

9. Smith, *Young Catholic America*, 10–13.

10. Smith, *Young Catholic America*, 15.

11. Smith, *Young Catholic America*, 17.

12. Peter Kreeft, "How to Win the Culture War," accessed March 30, 2020, http://www.peterkreeft.com/topics-more/how-to-win.htm.

13. J. Francis Cardinal Stafford, "The Year of Peirasmòs: 1968," Catholic News Agency, accessed September 2019, https://www.catholicnewsagency.com/resources/life-and-family/humanae-vitae/the-year-of-the-peirasms-1968.

14. Andrew Greely, *The Catholic Revolution: New Wine, Old Wineskins, and the Second Vatican Council* (University of California Press, 2004).

4. Letting Go of Unpracticed Preaching

1. Smith, *Young Catholic America*, 172.

2. Matthew Warner, "Why the World Doesn't Take Catholicism Seriously," *National Catholic Register*, May 15, 2013, https://www.ncregister.com/blog/matthew-warner/why-the-world-doesnt-take-catholicism-seriously.

5. Facing a Hypocritical Hierarchy

1. Anthony Thomas, "Secrets of the Vatican," *Frontline*, February 25, 2014, https://www.pbs.org/wgbh/frontline/film/secrets-of-the-vatican/transcript.

2. Robert Barron, *Letter to a Suffering Church* (Park Ridge, IL: Word on Fire, 2019), 6.

3. G. K. Chesterton, *Manalive* (New York: John Lane, 1912), 40.

4. David B. Barrett, George T. Kurian, and Todd M. Johnson, *World Christian Encyclopedia : A Comparative Survey of Churches and Religions in the Modern World*, 2nd ed. (New York: Oxford University Press, 2001).

6. Sorting Out the Heart of Sexuality

1. John Paul II, *Familiaris Consortio* (The Apostolic Exhortation on the Family), 11, November 22, 1981, http://www.vatican.va; *CCC*, 2361.

7. Digging into "Backward" Teachings

1. Paul VI, *Humanae Vitae* (Of Human Life), 17, July 25, 1968, http://www.vatican.va/content/paul-vi/en/encyclicals/documents/hf_p-vi_enc_25071968_humanae-vitae.html.

2. Lionel Tiger, *The Decline of Males: The First Look at an Unexpected New World for Men and Women* (New York: St. Martin's Griffin, 1999), 37–43.

3. Fulton J. Sheen, preface, in *Radio Replies*, by Charles Mortimer Carty and Leslie Rumble, vol. 1 (Charlotte, NC: Tan Books, 2012), ix.

8. Allowing Jesus to Make Us Happy

1. *God Is the Bigger Elvis*, directed by Rebecca Cammisa, aired April 1, 2012, on HBO, https://www.amazon.com/gp/video/detail/amzn1.dv.gti.ecac2ab7-b0fb-8569-69f1-812670bcd603?ref_=imdbref_tt_wbr_pvc_hbo&tag=imdbtag_tt_wbr_pvc_hbo-20.

2. Mindy Hecht, "The 613 Commandments (Mitzvot)," Chabad, accessed March 28, 2020, https://www.chabad.org/library/article_cdo/aid/756399/jewish/The-613-Commandments-Mitzvot.htm.

9. Embracing the Heroism of "Gloomy" Saints

1. C. S. Lewis, *The Weight of Glory* (New York: MacMillan, 1942), 2.

2. "Mother Teresa: Biographical," Nobel Prize, accessed April 28, 2020, https://www.nobelprize.org/prizes/peace/1979/teresa/biographical, from *Nobel Lectures: Peace 1971–1980*, ed. Tore Frängsmyr and Irwin Abrams (Singapore: World Scientific Publishing, 1997).

3. Fady Noun, "Mother Teresa, the War in Lebanon and the Rescue of 100 Orphans and Children with Disabilities," AsiaNews, September 2, 2016, http://www.asianews.it/news-en/Mother-Teresa%2C-the-war-in-Lebanon-and-the-rescue-of-100-orphans-and-children-with-disabilities-38470.html.

4. Maria Luisa Dagnino, *Bakhita: Saintly Daughter of Africa Tells Her Story*, English trans. ed. by Loretta Hall. (Gweru, Zimbabwe: Mambo Press, 1997).

Mallory Smyth is the content manager at Walking with Purpose. She previously worked as director of program growth for ENDOW and as a recruitment manager, development officer, and missionary for FOCUS.

Smyth earned a bachelor's degree in marketing from Louisiana State University. She has spoken at ENDOW and FOCUS conferences, including SEEK. Smyth has been a guest on EWTN and her writing has appeared in *Radiant* magazine. She lives in Littleton, Colorado, with her family.

www.mallory-smyth.com
Facebook: Mallory Bueche Smyth
Twitter: @malloryasmyth
Instagram: @malloryasmyth